Project
Leadership
from Theory to Practice

Project Leadership

from Theory to Practice

Jeffrey K. Pinto
Peg Thoms
Jeffrey Trailer
Todd Palmer
Michele Govekar

Project Management Institute

Library of Congress Cataloging-in-Publication Data

Project leadership: from theory to practice / Jeffrey K. Pinto ...
   [et al.].
         p.   cm.
      Includes bibliographical references (p.   ).
      ISBN: 1-880410-10-9 (pbk. : alk. paper)
      1. Industrial project management. 2. Teams in the workplace.
   3. Leadership. I. Pinto, Jeffrey K.
   HD69.P75P726 1998
   658.4'04 – – dc21   98–40611
                                                             CIP

Published by: Project Management Institute Headquarters
              Four Campus Boulevard, Newtown Square, Pennsylvania 19073-3299 USA
              Phone: 610-356-4600 or Visit our website: www.pmi.org

ISBN: 1-880410-10-9

PMI Book Team
Editor-in-Chief, James S. Pennypacker
Editor, Toni D. Knott
Assistant Editor, Lisa M. Fisher
Graphic Designer, Michelle T. Owen
Acquisitions Editor, Bobby R. Hensley
Production Coordinator, Mark S. Parker

10 9 8 7 6 5 4 3 2 1

Dedication

j.k.p. — To Joey, a wonderful surprise and ongoing joy.

p.t. — To Myke and Dave—my most important projects.

j.t. — To Flower, the Mouse, and the Bee, and to the crew of the USS Carl Vinson (CVN-70), who taught me hard lessons in leadership.

t.s.p. — To the best of the good old boys: TomBoy, Jethro Bodine, Big P, Big Daddy, Warren, and, of course, Jake the Snake.

m.g. — To the M.B.A students whose demand-pull approach demanded developing these ideas, the team of colleagues who knew we could, the spouse who read countless redrafts, and the Labrador retriever who put on many miles while I stretched my brain.

TABLE OF CONTENTS

LIST OF FIGURES

PREFACE

The importance of leadership in project management has long been acknowledged as one of the key ingredients for project success. Indeed, in a more general sense, the last few years have seen a tremendous resurgence of interest in this vital topic as books and articles explore in ever-increasing detail the various aspects and effects of leadership in organizations. These studies all point to the vital role that leadership plays in enhancing innovation, creativity, new product development, and competitiveness in an international marketplace.

Leadership is vital within the project management realm. Project managers play a key *lynchpin* role in their organizations, serving as the link between various stakeholder groups and working to create a strong and cohesive team atmosphere, all while maintaining budget and schedule constraints. Indeed, because of the essential centrality of project managers, many authors note that leadership skills are one of the most important qualities that managers can possess.

While there are currently a number of books on leadership in the popular and academic literatures, few such books attempt to develop a comprehensive understanding of the wide variety of leadership behaviors. That is, many such books focus on one or two critical components of leaders exclusively—for example, personality characteristics or team-building skills. Far rarer are the books that attempt to develop a more complete model of the role of the project leader in modern corporations, addressing such diverse but equally important roles as those of visionary, strategic manager, ethical leader, and so forth.

This book represents our attempt to develop a comprehensive, project management-oriented approach to project leadership. *Project Leadership: From Theory to Practice* is designed to fill an important and heretofore previously unexploited niche in the manager's bookshelf through presenting a practically written discussion of the important but diverse roles that leaders play and the impact that they have on successful project implementation. As the chapter titles indicate, we have developed a pragmatic guide to project leadership, making clear the direct links between general leadership theory and direct project management practice.

The idea for this book came about as the result of a team-taught course for the M.B.A. program at Penn State-Erie. Students had been increasingly interested in a course in applied leadership, and the management faculty members decided to pool their talents and create a course that was comprehensive (offering breadth), while focusing on gaining and applying leadership skills (intended to provide depth). Writing this book was a challenge in itself, as it required the collective efforts of five individuals to work in collaboration, to support and correct each other, and serve as both inspirational sources and critics of each other's efforts. It was truly a case of our having to live what we teach every day, through putting into practice the steps necessary to create effective teams.

APPROACH

Our approach is a combination of theory and practice. In the first chapters of the book, we lay a groundwork foundation, using some important guiding principles from the research on leadership and leader behavior, to put the idea of project leadership within its proper context. It was necessary to first demonstrate some of the relevant models of leadership before the reader can better understand the key role that leader behavior plays in successful project management. Once readers are led through the diverse duties and aspects of leadership behavior, they can better understand the comprehensive, ubiquitous nature of project leadership, learning to develop their leadership abilities in a variety of different but equally important dimensions. Our intention is to help project managers do a better job of running their projects through the valuable lessons that can be learned from understanding and applying the current state-of-the-art in research and practice on project leadership.

This book covers a variety of topics related to the study of project leadership. The first chapter will establish a framework of leadership in which we will demonstrate that *leading* is a multifaceted process, involving aspects of vision skills, ethical and political knowledge, strategic management and goal setting, and project team building. Following development of our full model, follow-on sections will explore each of these key areas in more detail, analyzing personality and trait theories of leadership, contingency models, and so on. Finally, we offer a concluding chapter, which offers some final, practical advice to project managers on how to make the most effective use of this information in developing or honing their own leadership styles.

In Summary

As we noted above, it is impossible to engage in a task of this nature without developing a keener sense of the importance of teamwork and leadership in any collective endeavor. Collaborations are always difficult because they comprise both the best and most difficult aspects of the writing process—gaining the advantage of multiple viewpoints while having to create a work in a purely consensual manner. That this book succeeded is due primarily to our desire to share the results of our experience in a pragmatic fashion. It is also the result, in no small part, of the success we have had in presenting similar material in a team-taught environment that has enabled us to appreciate more fully each other's work as teachers and scholars. We hope that project managers who read this work are left with a better understanding of the various perspectives of transformational project leadership and realize two other important points. First, that leadership training is a journey all can take (leadership behavior can be learned), and, second, we never completely arrive at our destination (there is always more to know). And so, the journey begins.

Jeffrey K. Pinto
Peg Thoms
Jeffrey Trailer
Todd S. Palmer
Michele Govekar

November 1997

CHAPTER 1

What Is Leadership?

SUSAN WAS NERVOUSLY watching the clock in her office as the hour slowly approached nine o'clock. Her first project staff meeting was about to begin. Three days ago, Susan had been named project manager for the newly initiated upgrade of one of her company's top-selling computer-networking software products. Susan has been with AtComm for three years and was recently promoted to a job as project manager in the New Products Division. Although she has had experience as an engineer on a number of projects since she joined AtComm, this will be her first opportunity to run a project on her own.

Susan slowly scanned the names on the list that she held: Phil Conrad from Sales and Marketing, Jonas Sutherland and Lois Robinson from Software Development, Ellen Holmes from Hardware Engineering, and Bill Winston from Systems Development. These five people were to comprise her core team, and she didn't know a thing about any of them.

"Typical," she thought, "my career is on the line here, and I have to depend on a group of total strangers."

Susan had had a meeting with her boss last week in which he told her that her project, initially budgeted at $1.5 million and with a six-month time frame, was viewed as one of the company's high-profile projects for the coming year. He also impressed on her the importance of hitting her target window. The product had to be launched on time, or AtComm would lose its competitive edge vis-à-vis its rivals. Everything she heard led Susan to believe that her performance on this project would go far toward moving her up the corporate ladder or propelling her out the front door.

Now, as she waited for the staff meeting to get under way, Susan reviewed everything she knew about her new job. The key, she was convinced, would be her ability to develop her core team into an integrated unit. She knew enough about project management to know that it required a team's commitment to be done well.

How would she gain that commitment? What could she do to get the project moving on the right foot? How could she lead when she knew so little about leadership?

The abrupt knock on her office door brought an end to these ruminations and announced the beginning of her project staff meeting. ✸

I WANT TO BE A COWBOY: THE LEADERSHIP MYTH

We all want to be cowboys, and why not? Cowboys have always held a special place in our hearts. When we are kids, we point our fingers, yell *bang,* and then argue for hours whether we are dead or just wounded. When we grow up, who has not daydreamed of hogtieing her overbearing boss and riding off into the sunset to the cheers of coworkers? Cowboys are resourceful, daring, and are as quick with their wits as they are with their fists. They are always right. They always win.

In many ways, we see cowboys as the embodiment of leadership. Business leaders, like cowboys, are often presented as mythical figures doing amazing things. Standing alone and apart from ordinary folks, they are dreamers perched upon their mustangs, making their plans as they gaze off into a lonesome moon. Yet, when the time comes for action, they dig their spurs into their horses' sides, gallop down to the town people, and tell them to circle the wagons. There they are, at the front of the fight, with their six-guns blazing, dropping the vermin dead in their tracks. And when the battle is over, off they go riding into the sunset to receive their rewards—the school marm for the cowboy, stock options for executives.

Of course, the problem is that life is not a John Wayne horse opera. We know this. For most of the hundreds of things that we do every day at work, we have a realistic view of what is expected and what is required. Most managers do not go into cloud-cuckoo-land when contemplating quality, deadlines, performance appraisals, strategic planning, and so on. But, when it comes to leadership, most of us jump back on our horses and head right back to the range (where the deer and the antelope play).

Problems arise when the myth of the leader becomes the end-all and the be-all of our learning processes. If we buy into a myth that is so overpowering, how can we ever hope to become one with our dreams? The result is that too many of us look at these ideals as something unobtainable. You have to be born a leader. You can never *become* one.

In no other area of management education is the concept of myth as prevailing as in leadership. We have all seen the books down at the local bookstore: *The Twenty-Seven Habits of Semi-Effective People, The Leadership Secrets of a Fascist Dictator, The One Nanosecond Manager*, and so on. Each claims to sell the secret of life, to impart unto you the magic word to make you a leader. Part of the problem arises in the use of terminology. *Vision*, for example, may lead one more often to think of Moses than of everyday business activity. But perhaps the larger problem crops up when people start talking about myths; they often have no idea what they are talking about. Myths are ways of simplifying our universe. Sometimes we simplify so much that myth and reality are no longer on speaking terms.

2

For example, cowboys do have a lot to teach us about leadership but not the cowboys that we are used to. What do cowboys do? Lead cows. Have you ever seen anything that indicates that John Wayne knows how to lead cows? What would he do? Go to the front of the herd and yell, "Charge"? Or perhaps just punch the lead cow in the face? What about Roy Rogers? Would he yodel until the cows moved or threaten to stuff them like he did to old Trigger? Obviously, Roy and the Duke are great Hollywood cowboys. They ride horses, shoot guns, and always get the girl. But have you ever seen them with a cow? Would you want them around a cow? Your cow?

Go behind the myth, and true leadership characteristics emerge. A herd of cows is a lot like an organization: massive and, at times, rather aimless. It takes dedicated leadership using a score of methods to energize this bovine bulk. A good cowboy knows how to select a lead cow, direct the herd into natural flows, and rely upon his well-trained subordinate, his horse, to help lead the herd. Moving a herd into Dodge City required considerable skill. It is the real cowboy, not a stylized caricature, that teaches us something about leadership.

Likewise, when examining leadership from the business perspective, one should view many of the myths about this subject with a grain of salt (a ten- or fifteen-pound grain should suffice!). Nobody can teach you leadership with a four-by-four diagram. Rather, it is a time-consuming and engaging task, requiring a great deal of thought and resources.

The book you are holding is not a cookbook. You will find no recipes for *leadership stew* here. Rather, this book is intended as a guide to leadership thought and practice. It is premised upon the following principles.

- Good theory underlies good leadership. Theory has received a bad *rap*. After all, we want doers, not thinkers, right? But, at its heart, leadership is concerned with transforming ideas and concepts into action. Your knowledge of basic principles is essential to you taking the first step to being an effective leader. In many ways it is like playing baseball. The difference between a good and a great hitter is the ability to *think through* the ball, to anticipate the ball's path and trajectory. Good, consistent hitting is more a matter of understanding the underlying principles than possessing a strong arm.
- Focus on leadership, not leaders. A lot of people make claims to being leaders. Every day, the bookstores are filled with badly written, much ballyhooed books by CEOs proclaiming their leadership brilliance. Yet, what they attribute to their leadership, many others would more accurately link to sound managerial skills, first-mover advantage, industry structure, and just good, old-fashioned luck. Just because a person succeeds does not mean that what he did can be ascribed to leadership skills. And this is the reason why focusing on leaders can often lead to the wrong conclusions. Also, it can be difficult translating one

person's life experiences to assist another. Alexander the Great was a great leader, yet to try and understand his life and then transfer wholesale the principles upon which he built his kingdom would be dangerous.

▪ Leadership can be exercised daily. Leaders can only come into their own during extraordinary times, à la Lee Iacocca, right? Wrong. Leadership is a day-in and day-out activity. To insist that leadership is exceptional or above the norm condemns us to situations in which we can never develop leadership skills. Then, when the extraordinary does happen, we are set up to fail because we have had no opportunities to learn, to test our wings.

▪ Leadership can be developed. At the heart of leadership is a set of skills that can be honed and cultivated through insightful self-discovery. Furthermore, managers can make attitudinal adjustments through the visioning process (described in Chapters 4 and 5). With patience, leadership can be developed as much as any other managerial activity.

The quest for better leadership practices in managing projects is one that remains a compelling motivation in one company after another around the globe. More and more organizations are using project management as a key tool for implementing a variety of strategic organizational moves, including everything from new product development to new systems installations. Indeed, as many readers are aware, project management has literally taken off in the past decade. Companies are beginning to understand how effective project management allows them to operate both more efficiently and capably in their competitive environments. At the same time, however, these organizations are coming to realize that while it is an effective technique, project management requires a tremendous commitment from the organization if it is to be done appropriately.

One of the keys to successful project management has always been strong, incisive leadership. Project management is a *leader-intensive* undertaking, meaning that, for it to be successful, project management requires the efforts of individuals willing to engage in the numerous and diverse activities needed to promote project success. Successful projects, as we all know, simply do not *happen*. They are the result of the collective energies of a number of key project team members and stakeholders. None of these members is more important to project success than the project manager, operating as the project's leader, in every sense of the word.

If leadership is so important for project success, why is so little written about it within the project management arena? Part of the answer to that question comes from the fact that we are still learning about the various aspects of leadership. The field itself is continually evolving as we come more and more to understand the wide manner of ways in which leadership can affect project success. A second reason, closely tied to the first, has to do with the difficulty of coming to grips with the concept of leadership. It seems that when we refer to someone as a *leader*, there is a natural potential to ascribe a wide variety of different meanings to the term. In other words, if we cannot agree on what a leader is, how are we to promote effective leadership in our project management organizations?

THE NATURE OF LEADERSHIP

Few words evoke as much imagery or provoke as many varied interpretations as *leadership* does. While we often assign leadership abilities to captains of industry, heads of political or military organizations, and other equally highly visible individuals, in fact leaders emerge in all facets of our daily lives. People serving on school boards or with charity organizations possess the same qualities of leadership as their more well-publicized counterparts. As a topic of research and publishing, leadership is equally popular. It has been estimated that over thirty thousand articles and books have been written on leadership and leader behavior in this century alone (DuBrin 1995). A word search over the Internet, using *leadership*, generated over 309,000 responses. Clearly, leadership has become a well-used part of our everyday vocabularies.

With all that has been written and discussed about leadership, do we have any sense of an underlying definition of the term? While a number of working definitions of leadership exist, some that illustrate both the nature of leadership and the duties of leaders include the following (Bass 1990):

- using our interpersonal influence on team members to attain organizational and personal goals
- having the ability to generate a compelling collective vision and communicate it in a way that motivates others
- acting in a way that causes others to respond in a shared direction.

What are the common themes running though these definitions? Clearly, they suggest that leaders possess a vision of the future, a sense of where they see themselves, their team, and the organization. Having a vision, however, is useless without the concomitant ability to communicate it in an effective manner to others. We can either lead by example or through establishing a message so compelling that it motivates compliance. Further, leaders understand the art of influence—the ability to initiate actions in others, regardless of respective ranks within the company. The goal of leaders, it has been said, is to produce change.

Through the vision of future possibilities and their efforts toward creating collective action, they work to change the status quo, to move their organizations or their teams in new and challenging directions in pursuit of their goals.

Leaders are goal directed. As we will demonstrate in later chapters, leadership behavior does not consist simply of taking care of one's team. Certainly there is a strong need to consider the project team members' feelings and attitudes, working to keep job satisfaction and motivation high. At the same time, however, effective leaders also understand that they must remain mission driven. Their goal is the successful completion of a project. The steps they take, both for the welfare of the team and the pursuit of the project's goals, are all aimed at successful project implementation.

TRANSFORMATIONAL VERSUS TRANSACTIONAL LEADERSHIP

One method for understanding the unique characteristics of effective project leaders is to examine the difference between two distinct forms of leadership: transactional and transformational. The term, *transactional leaders*, typically refers to those individuals who view their jobs as a series of discrete transactions between themselves and their subordinates. They generally are good administrators in that they operate as problem solvers. Because they deal with issues as they come up (transactions), they may be excessively reactive rather than inclined to develop a vision for themselves, their departments, or their projects.

Transformational leaders, on the other hand, seek to make their mark on the organization or their projects through operating in a forward-thinking, often charismatic, manner. They work to make a difference as project managers, through transforming their project teams and, ultimately, their projects, in positive ways. We will argue throughout this book that a transformational leadership model is very appropriate for successful project managers. They must learn to view their work as a challenge of transformation—taking a chaotic and disorderly situation (the beginning of a new project) and, through their personal energy and ability to inspire team members, creating a vision of project success that motivates high commitment from the team.

When we consider some of the characteristics of transformational leaders, it is easy to see how they apply to successful project management. As readers will see, these themes resonate throughout this text. Briefly, transformational leaders have the following attributes (DuBrin 1995).

- Vision—Transformational project leaders are vision-driven individuals. Unlike transactional, reactive project managers, successful project leaders offer their teams and stakeholders an exciting view of where the project is headed, its goals, and potential. A vision, representing the ideal state of project success, gives the team a rallying point and a goal to strive for throughout the project's development.
- Good communication skills—It makes no sense to have a vision of the future if we are unable to communicate that vision to our teams. Successful project leaders understand that at the hub of all effective project activity lies the ability to communicate, inspire, instruct, and inform.
- Ability to inspire trust—A recent study by two noted experts on leadership found after interviewing thousands of managers that the number-one characteristics possessed by effective leaders were honesty and trustworthiness (Kouzes and Posner 1995). Transformational leaders' greatest legacy is often the fact that their team members will risk their own careers to support the project leader's vision.
- Ability to empower—Effective leaders make their team members feel capable. They build rather than constantly tear down. Transformational leaders understand that it is not just the project's success by which they are measured but their ability to develop team members to their fullest potential.
- Energy and action orientation—Transformational leaders are characterized by high levels of personal energy and enthusiasm. Indeed, they understand that it is impossible to inspire others if they themselves are lethargic or lukewarm in their reactions to their latest challenge.
- Emotional expressiveness and warmth—Most transformational leaders are able to express their feelings openly. They do not leave their team constantly guessing about their latest mood; they do not play their cards close to the chest. Team members are not constantly tiptoeing around them in fear of explosions. These leaders know that they are expected to play cheerleader.
- Willingness to take personal risks—Transformational leaders share a common characteristic with successful entrepreneurs: they are not risk averse. In leading by personal example, they understand that if they expect their teams to use dynamic and potentially untried (risky) approaches to solve project-related problems, then they must exhibit similar attitudes.
- Use of unconventional strategies—A common term coming up in business these days is expressed as a willingness to *think outside the box*. What this phrase refers to is an attitude of refusing to be bound by conventional thinking and programmed decision-making. Thinking outside the box shows the project team that creativity and nontraditional thinking are encouraged and rewarded.

Figure 1. Elements Involved in Successful Project Operations

Vision (1) of the leader guides the direction of the project by imagining what the completed project will produce.

Strategy (2) reminds us to maintain an awareness of the project's fit into the larger context.

Ethics (2, 5) guide the actions of the leader and establish a positive project environment.

Team Building (2, 4, 5) guides the evolution and the development of a high-performing project team.

Classical Theories (1, 2, 3, 4, 5) identify the general characteristics found to be important in effective leadership.

Accountability (1, 2, 3, 4, 5) guides the leader's use of reward power to create a productive project environment.

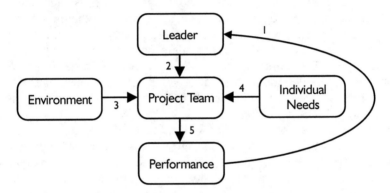

- Self-promoting personality—Transformational leaders are not shy; they do not hide their lights under bushels. Successful project managers understand the importance of playing the key political games, using influence and self-promotion to advance their projects. Transformational leaders have many characteristics; reticence, however, is not one of them.
- Capable in crises—True leadership is difficult to assess when things run smoothly. Projects, as we know, rarely do. In fact, it is precisely in how project managers handle the myriad problems of a typical project that we find the greatest measure of their leadership abilities. Transformational leaders rise to the challenge, seeing opportunity where others see only threat.

This book is organized around the unifying theme of transformational leadership. As Figure 1 demonstrates, we view project leaders' actions as essentially the result of a number of issues, including their personal leadership styles, visioning ability, and understanding of team and personal accountability. Although the chapters will develop these points in considerable detail, they suggest that some of the most well-known leadership actions—including inspiring and building effective project teams, using influencing skills, and so forth—are directly related to our understanding of leader characteristics.

Transformational project leadership requires readers to understand at the outset that we are not offering a set of freestanding and independent leadership characteristics that can be adopted, or not, as the reader is inclined. Rather, leadership behavior is an integrated whole, based on possessing or developing both underlying personal characteristics and understanding their impact through applying specific leader behaviors. Attempting to develop one side of the model without the other is fruitless. It is no more possible to manifest leadership actions without understanding their underlying causes than we would be inclined to refine our leadership abilities to their highest potential without ever testing them by putting these theories into action.

Leadership behavior can be acquired. Despite the opinions of some that leadership is an innate personality characteristic that some have, and the majority do not, research and practical experience demonstrate quite clearly that this is not so. It is possible for all project managers to improve their leadership styles, first, through a clearer understanding of their preferred methods for running projects.

THE UNIFYING NATURE OF LEADERSHIP

Leadership behavior exists at the heart of successful project development. Having made this point, it is necessary to look at precisely how leader behavior affects all aspects of project implementation. Figure 1 illustrates the various elements involved in successful project operations, arguing that the combination of both internal and external environments, leader behavior, and an understanding of individual team members' needs all can positively or negatively influence project team development. This team development will have a direct effect on the resultant project performance.

As a unifying theme, Figure 1 also demonstrates the linkages between the various chapters developed in this book. In order to understand the nature of the leadership challenge, it is important to devote some time to explaining the various models of leadership—which ones apply to the project management process, how they relate to each other, their practical implications, and so forth. Chapter 2 will take the reader through a short survey of important leadership ideas. We suggest that even though *theory* has gotten something of a bad reputation, implying somehow that it must therefore be divorced from reality, a solid grounding in basic leadership theories will go far toward making the ideas presented in this book clear and immediately applicable.

The important underlying theme of these theories is presented in our chapter on accountability. All leadership is a balancing act; it consists of an implicit understanding that we have to find the appropriate balance between an all-out desire for task accomplishment and an equally strong need to nurture and develop our team. This chapter will demonstrate the problems with an overemphasis on either philosophy. Too-high task concern may turn us into autocratic, insensitive monsters. On the other hand, an excessive focus on our team members and their feelings can lead to projects wallowing in uncompleted inertia, as we never seem to have the ability to drive the task to completion. Creating accountability is our desire as project leaders to find a middle ground working with and developing team members, but only within a strict set of project guidelines.

At the heart of leader behavior is the ability to develop the unique vision for the project that guides its direction. Project vision means an a priori understanding (and ability to communicate) what the completed project will resemble, the problems it will solve, and the benefits it will provide. An anonymous wit once noted that, "any road will get you there if you don't know where you are going." Vision gives the leader the ability to project a positive and defined message to the project team and relevant stakeholders. Chapters 4 and 5 discuss the importance of and practical steps involved in developing a clear project vision and communicating it effectively to team members.

Because any *leader* only operates within the context of his team, it is clear that team-building abilities are key to effective project leadership. Team building acknowledges some important truths about successful project implementation: 1) It can only come about as the result of a motivated, integrated project team, and 2) *Teams* do not happen by accident. Successful projects occur as the result of successful teamwork. Competent and effective interactions among team members sound much easier in theory than they are in real life. The truth, as many readers will attest, is that taking a diverse group of individuals, usually with different functional backgrounds, experiences, and training, and molding them into a cohesive unit is one of project management's greatest challenges. It does not happen naturally or by chance. This metamorphosis occurs through careful preparation, understanding of human and team-related needs, and a knowledge of our own leadership style.

Embedded in effective leadership is the ethical side of our decision processes. Research has suggested that one of the traits most people look for in leaders is a sense of honesty or integrity (Kouzes and Posner 1995). This basic honesty implies that we are using our leadership for positive means, through creating an atmosphere for project development that encourages the best from each team member. In this sense, ethics is not simply an add-on feature to leadership—"Sure we want good leaders. Oh, and if they can be honest too, that would be nice."—it is a key component of the leadership function.

The chapter on strategy and leadership brings into focus the sense that all projects are effective to the degree that we have made them fit into the larger environmental context. History abounds with examples of *successful* projects that did not fit the organizational context and, hence, were abandoned as expensive white elephants. Oregon's Department of Transportation recently spent millions to develop a computerized automobile-registration system that was only belatedly found to be so flawed, both in its technical snags and conceptual misunderstandings, that it was simply abandoned as a very expensive write-off. In the chapter, we offer some guidelines for project managers to make sure that while their projects are on the developmental track, their underlying strategies are still appropriate; in other words, the engine driving the project is still moving in the correct direction.

Writing a book on project leadership is an ambitious undertaking. Yet, based on our years of research, personal project management experiences, consulting, and interview data, it is clear that too much is at stake on both personal and organizational levels with our projects to go into them without a clear view of what effective leadership can do for a project's chances for success. Every reader can easily recall examples within their own organizations of projects that both succeeded and bombed due, in large part, to the actions or errors of the project leader.

At the heart of many people's difficulties with exercising leadership is our misunderstanding of what leadership means. Once we start to *demythologize* leadership, to make the term understandable and accessible to all, we take the first step toward opening up great opportunities for a number of novice project managers, scared to death at the thought of their first step into the live-fire range of project management. This book is another sort of *first step*. It represents a first step at stripping away the veil of mystique surrounding leadership, making it easier for project managers to both understand and practice. And that is the most important first step of all.

CHAPTER 2

Classical Theories of Leadership

A GOOD MAGICIAN is a good theorist. Compare the elegant conjuring of David Copperfield to the fumblings of your neighbor's ten-year-old son showing you his newly learned tricks from his Great Zookini Junior Magic Kit. It is more than just technical proficiency and subtle handwork that propels you into the sorcerer's magical realm of transmuting doves and endless pitchers of milk. Rather, it is the magician's understanding and application of the basic principles of manipulating his audience that allow you to suspend your belief so that he then can levitate you right out of your seat.

Leadership, like magic, is based upon a similar understanding. Your comprehension of basic leadership theory is essential for your growth and potential as a leader. The trick, so to speak, is that your understanding of theory should be so deeply ingrained in your psyche that its application appears casual. A mark of great magicians is that their efforts appear to be effortless! If you see some cut-rate Houdini struggling to make the cards jump from his hands, then you refuse to admit him to that special place in your mind that allows you to suspend your belief. It is that suspension of belief that is the real trick of a great magician.

As with the Zookini Junior Magic Kit, this chapter will not make you a great leader. Yet, it is only through an understanding of these theories and their possible applications that true leadership can result. Leadership, like magic, is premised on some rather basic principles. Both the Great Blackstone and your neighbor's kid essentially employ the same bag of tricks. But the results can be markedly different. When Blackstone saws a woman in half, we rise to our feet in cheers. When your neighbor's kid attempts the same trick, we rise to our feet to dial 9-1-1.

For project managers, the need to understand these theories and their possible applications is vital. The problem, as in much of project management, is that you have only a limited amount of time to exert leadership. As a result, many managers are like your Uncle Ned at the all-you-can-eat salad bar at the Sizzler, loading your plate with a little bit of everything, without a true appreciation for any of it.

The focus of this book is on the transformational model of leadership. But other theories can obviously give us invaluable perspective. In order to help us understand these theories, we have divided them into four basic groups that focus on the leader aspects or the situational aspects of leadership. (A model to understand models—now we are cooking with gas!) We can look at leader aspects through either traits or behaviors. We can examine situations from the perspective of whether they are universal or contingent upon specific situations and personalities. Our goal is to create perspective, to give the reader a framework for understanding these theories within a larger context. It is important to remember that they are not necessarily competing theories. We can get maximum benefit from understanding how each approach complements the others. Together, they offer a powerful theoretical look at leadership—theoretical, yes, but also practical. After all, no competent magician ever sealed himself in a milk container about to be submerged in water until he had his theory down pat!

CONTINGENT LEADERSHIP THEORIES

The premise of contingency theories is that optimal leadership is achieved only by synthesizing the requirements of the situation with the leader: either by matching the leader to the situation, or by matching leader behavior to the situation. In either case, these theories offer the identification and assessment of situation factors, which are necessary toward explaining effective leadership. We will discuss contingent leader-behavior theories and a contingent leader-trait theory.

CONTINGENT BEHAVIOR THEORIES

The common premise of these theories is that leadership improves as the *fit* between leader behavior and the needs of the situation are optimized. These approaches assume that leader behavior can be adapted to the situation, and that, therefore, these theories have a strong potential for developing and improving leadership. Three of these theories are discussed—Situational Leadership, Path Goal Theory, and the Vroom-Jago Model—and the discussion is concluded with the Bonoma-Slevin-Pinto leadership model, which synthesizes and simplifies the contributions of these approaches to help the project manager choose a leadership style that *fits* the situation.

Figure 2.   Leader and Situation Aspects of Leadership

	Situational Aspects	
Leader Aspects	Contingent	Universal
Behavior	Situational Leadership Path-Goal Leadership Vroom-Jago Model	Leadership Grid®
Traits	Least Preferred Co-Worker (LPC)	Charismatic Leadership Transformational Leadership

Adapted from Jago, 1982.

Situational Leadership®

In this theory, the two important dimensions of leader behavior are *relationship behavior* and *task behavior*. The important characteristic of the situation is follower (i.e., project team member) *maturity*:

■ relationship behavior—leader actions that demonstrate a concern for people; facilitating participation in decision-making, coaching, sharing ideas, explaining decisions, and so on

■ task behavior—leader actions that emphasize a concern for the task; clarifying procedures, duties, responsibilities, and so on

■ follower maturity—the readiness of the follower is determined by assessing ability to perform the task and motivation to perform the task. The motivation of the follower is predominately associated with the general willingness to perform or confidence in the ability to perform.

LEADERSHIP STYLES FOR AN OPTIMAL *FIT*

The optimal leadership style is argued to be driven by both the characteristics of the job and psychological readiness, or maturity, of the individual (see Figure 3). Action by the leader with respect to task behavior is argued to vary according to the level of follower maturity with respect to the job: when a team member lacks experience (maturity is low), leader involvement is necessary, and task-oriented behavior should be a priority. As the follower gains experience and confidence with respect to the task, the need for intervention by the leader falls to the point when, ultimately, the follower is acting autonomously. Correspondingly, leader relationship-oriented behavior is argued to vary according to the level of

Figure 3.   Situational Leadership Model

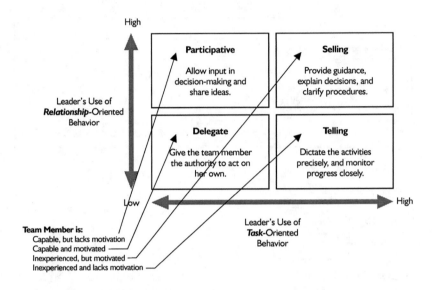

Adapted from Hersey and Blanchard, 1988.

the follower's confidence and ability (psychological maturity). High levels of relationship-oriented behavior by the project leader are appropriate only for medium levels of team member psychological maturity.

Categorized as leadership styles, the four general levels of maturity and their corresponding leader behaviors are described as telling, selling, participating, and delegating.

- Telling—Team members, who lack required abilities and confidence or motivation to perform, require intervention by the project leader. The team member requires clear instruction as to how to effectively perform but is considered unlikely to accept coaching. Thus, the optimal project leadership style involves only high levels of task-oriented behavior.
- Selling—Team members, who lack required abilities, yet are motivated to perform, require instruction as to how to effectively perform and will likely accept coaching. Thus, the optimal leadership style includes high levels of task- and relationship-oriented behavior.
- Participating—Team members with strong ability, who lack the motivation to perform, do not require instruction on the task but require intervention by the project leader to increase their confidence or will-

ingness to perform. Thus, the optimal leadership style includes high levels of relationship-oriented behavior only.

■ Delegating—Team members with strong ability and strong motivation to perform do not require extensive intervention by the leader. The team member may find such intervention an insult, as it implies that she is not capable or motivated when, in fact, she is. Thus, the optimal project leadership style is to avoid interfering with the team member by delegating the task.

The major contribution of this approach is in identifying an important situation variable, *follower maturity*, and presenting an argument as to why an imbalance in leader behavior in favor of either concern for the task or concern for people is functional. Note that this is in general modifies the leadership grid argument for an unbalanced emphasis approach.

Path-Goal Theory

The premise is that leadership is the ability to clarify the follower's path to his goal. The premise is based on the expectancy theory of work motivation, which holds that motivation of an individual team member is determined by his assessment of three things: 1) the likelihood that he can successfully complete the given task; 2) the likelihood that successful completion of the task will be rewarded; and 3) the meaningfulness of the reward to the team member. Thus, when the individual perceives that the task can be completed and will be rewarded, and the reward is meaningful, the individual will be motivated to perform. Consequently, the leader can play an important role in facilitating the team's attainment of organization goals by:

■ taking actions to increase the team members' perceptions that they can complete their tasks

■ ensuring that team members are consistently rewarded

■ modifying the type of rewards to fit the needs of the individual members.

Based on this argument, four generic styles of leadership are identified to be appropriate to most situations: directive, supportive, participative, and achievement oriented.

Directive. This comprises leader actions that emphasize clarifying the means of task accomplishment: structuring activities, coordinating, planning, organizing, controlling, and so on. This is an autocratic leader approach, which is most appropriate when the team members lack experience. The idea is to build the team members' confidence that their efforts will result in successful completion of the task. Clearly, for project managers, this approach can only work when project leaders possess sufficient technical expertise so that they can involve themselves in the day-to-day development activities of the project. When the project leader is a generalist, or unfamiliar with the specific technical aspects of the development process, directive leadership is inappropriate.

Supportive. In this style, leader actions are predominantly concerned with maximizing the welfare of the team members. This style is most appropriate when the task is stressful, boring, tedious, and generally dissatisfying, or when team members have a high fear of failure. The purpose is to modify the task structure and the type of rewards to best meet the individual needs of the team members. This requires actions that open communication to gain an awareness and understanding of the team members' values.

Participative. This style involves leader actions that provide team members with the opportunity to contribute to the decision-making process. This democratic leadership style is most appropriate when tasks are nonroutine, the team members have a high level of technical knowledge, and the team members are well motivated. The idea is to increase the team members' commitment and expectations that their efforts will lead to successful task accomplishment through participation in decisions on task structure and goals.

Achievement Oriented. This type of leadership comprises leader actions that focus on challenging the team: setting high standards, delegating responsibility for the work, and so on. This style is most appropriate when the task is unstructured, and the competence of the team members is high. The idea is to increase the meaningfulness of the team members' accomplishments by emphasizing the intrinsic rewards of success in a challenging environment. Many examples exist of project development in high-tech organizations in which team members are motivated by the technical challenges rather than by external directives. Wise project managers in these environments routinely rely on achievement-oriented actions to encourage their team members to meet these challenges with as little interference from the project manager as possible.

Vroom-Jago Model

The premise of this leadership model is that project leaders can improve team performance through increased goal acceptance, commitment, and task motivation when followers participate in the decision process. In other words, the greater the team members' participation in goal development, the greater their buy-in to the development process. The problem of how much involvement and under what circumstances participation should occur is the focus of the model. The solution to determining optimal participation is achieved by first delineating the leader's alternative methods for structuring the follower's participation in the decision. Second, the important situation variables are defined, and third, a decision tree is provided that shows the leader how to select among the alternative decision-participation methods based on the leader's assessment of each of the situational variables.

The types of decision methods in Figure 4 reflect not only a range of participation by the subordinates but also a range of time necessary for the decision methods. We assume that the levels of participation determine the amount of time required for making the decision; higher participation requires more time. Thus, decisions that are constrained by time should be more autocratic. Alternatively, it is assumed that participation in the decision-making process is an important element in the development of the subordinate, as well as in creating a basis for building trust, commitment, and so on. Thus, decision-making should be more participative or democratic when the decision is not time critical. The incorporation of these situational attributes is the primary improvements of the Vroom-Jago decision model over the original Vroom-Yetton model.

The major limitation of the Vroom-Jago model is the difficulty for the novice in using the model pragmatically. This model is the most complex of the classical theories presented, and this can make it impractical for general use unless the leader devotes the serious study time necessary to internalize the rules in a way that allows the leader to assess the situation and structure optimal participation quickly from memory.

Choosing Your Leadership Style

Given that we, the project managers, are willing and able to consciously choose a leadership style to fit the situation, we would benefit from a model that simplifies the manner in which we assess the situations we find ourselves in. The model presented in Figure 5 illustrates two dimensions of project management situations found to be critical in choosing our leadership style: information input, and decision authority.

■ Information input: When we are making a decision, large amounts of information from the team may be required in order to make a properly informed choice. When this situation arises, we seek high levels of input from the team, and we can follow one of two leadership styles: consensus, where we allow the team to make the decision; or consultative autocrat, where we absorb the input but make the ultimate decision ourselves. Conversely, there are decisions that require little, if any, input from the team to make a properly informed choice. In this situation, we can choose from two alternative leadership styles: autocrat, where we make the decision alone; or shareholder, where we allow the team to make the decision. In each of these situations, the proper level of decision authority is the critical means of deciding which leadership style is best.

Figure 4.   Vroom/Yetton and Vroom/Jago Models

Vroom/Yetton Model

Symbol	Definition
AI	You make the decision yourself using the information available to you at the present time.
AII	You collect the required information from subordinates and then make the decision yourself. You may or may not share the purpose of your questions with subordinates. Subordinates do not help define the problem, or generate and evalutate alternative solutions.
CI	You present the problem, individually, to the relevant subordinates, then *you* make the decision, which may or may not reflect their influence.
CII	You present the problem to subordinates in a group meeting, obtaining their ideas and suggestions. Then *you* make the decision, which may or may not reflect your subordinates' influence.
GII	You present the problem to your subordinates as a group. Together you generate and evaluate alternatives, with a goal of reaching a consensus on the best solution. You coordinate the discussion, keeping it focused, and making sure that the relevant, critical issues are discussed. You provide the group with information and ideas that you have, but without pushing them to adopt your solution. You must be willing to accept and implement any solution that has the support of the entire group.

Vroom/Jago Model

Decision Tree Governing Group Decision Problems

A.   Is a HIGH-QUALITY decision required?

B.   Is the INFORMATION SUFFICIENT to make a high-quality decision?

C.   Is this a STRUCTURED decision problem?

D.   In order to achieve EFFECTIVE IMPLEMENTATION, is it important that subordinates accept the decision?

E.   Would SUBORDINATES ACCEPT the decision if you were to make the decision yourself?

F.   Are the ORGANIZATIONAL GOALS to be achieved in solving this problem consistent with the SUBORDINATES' GOALS?

G.   Is it likely that SUBORDINATES will DISAGREE on preferred solutions?

H.   Is the decision driven more by the need to DEVELOP SUBORDINATES, rather than time constraints? (Avoid AI, AII, CI)

I.   Are the subordinates DISPERSED GEOGRAPHICALLY? (Avoid CII, GII)

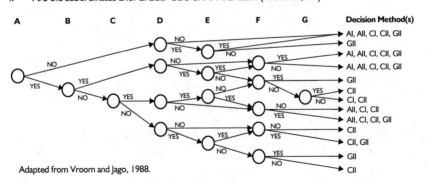

Adapted from Vroom and Jago, 1988.

Figure 5. Slevin/Pinto Model

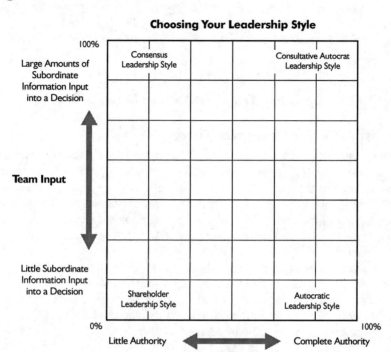

Choosing Your Leadership Style

Adapted from Slevin and Pinto, 1991.

■ Decision authority: The authority to make a decision can be retained by the project manager or delegated to the team. That is, every decision made by the project manager implicitly carries with it the need to choose a level of decision authority. Project managers who choose to retain complete authority to make the decision maximize speed and control but deny team members the opportunity to develop their decision-making skills and to influence the project. Project managers who delegate complete decision authority improve motivation of the team by allowing them to contribute, but this tends to lower the project manager's coordination and control of the project.

The tradeoffs associated with allowing different levels of information input and decision authority create an opportunity for the project leader to choose a leadership style that *fits* the situation. Thus, it is important that we assess ourselves: Do you tend to maintain one style regardless of the situation? Are you willing to delegate decision authority? Do you always delegate decision authority? Do you allow the team to provide input to project decisions? To the extent that we are inflexible on these two important issues, we are missing opportunities to improve our project leadership. The goal, then, is to be proactively flexible in our approach to decision-making and learn to consciously choose our leadership style.

CONTINGENT TRAIT APPROACH TO LEADERSHIP

Least Preferred Coworker Theory

The power of contingency theory is that the effectiveness of a leader is determined by the *fit* between a leader's personal style and the potential for control in the work situation. By identifying the important personality and situational variables, the organization can maximize effective leadership by matching the leader to the situation. Accordingly, the dominant personality characteristic is argued to be the leader's coworker preferences.

Leader Style. Least preferred coworker (LPC) measures the leader's hierarchy of needs; high LPC indicates that the leader's satisfaction is driven primarily by positive, successful interpersonal relationships; task achievement is the dominant motivation indicated by a low LPC score.

Situation Control. The important leadership situation characteristic is the extent to which the leader can control and coordinate the work. Three dimensions of control are measured.

- Position power—measures the magnitude of the leader's authority: hiring, firing, promotion, demotion, and so on. Greater position power is argued to indicate greater control over the tasks.
- Task structure—measures the extent to which the means of accomplishing tasks are known and well defined. Highly structured tasks are argued to facilitate high levels of control.
- Leader-member relations—measures the extent to which interpersonal relationships are positive and functional. Strong relations are argued to indicate trust, commitment, and respect between the leader and the subordinates. This facilitates higher levels of control in that subordinates will react more positively and quickly to direction from a trusted leader.

UNIVERSAL LEADERSHIP BEHAVIOR

Universal leadership behavior theories argue that certain behaviors enhance leadership in all situations. This approach to leadership is helpful in *developing* project leaders because it assumes that individuals can modify their behavior to become better leaders. The model provides a generic leadership-behavior baseline, or standard, against which the individual can compare her own behaviors. This comparison enables the individual to detect personal discrepancies from optimal behavior, allowing adjustment of subsequent behavior to improve leadership effectiveness. Thus, the focus of this section is to gain an awareness of universal behaviors that have been found to be important for leaders.

The Leadership Grid

The premise of the leadership grid is that effective leader behavior falls into two generic categories: concern for people, and concern for production. Only by actively demonstrating a concern for both can the leader maximize team performance.

- Concern for people—involves leader-initiated actions that enhance the trust and respect between the leader and the subordinate. Generally, this involves actions that help the subordinates meet their personal goals. Such actions concern the social and growth needs of the subordinate but also include actions to maximize the quality of work-life: issues such as ensuring that their compensation is fair, their job is secure, their work environment is safe and comfortable, and so on.
- Concern for production—involves leader-initiated behaviors that increase the output of the team. Generally, this involves actions that meet the performance goals of the firm: increasing efficiency, volume, quality, and so on.

Leaders often fail to emphasize both because personality traits or personal skills and abilities make leaders more adept at one category of leader behavior than the other, and they are therefore reluctant to initiate behaviors in which they lack confidence and efficiency. Some project managers are good at team development but are afraid to *crack the whip* when necessary. Others may be highly task oriented but suffer from an inability to understand or foster much personal concern for the welfare of their teams. Through self-assessment exercises, the leadership grid offers a means of identifying and correcting neglected behaviors.

The dominant limitation of this approach is the general vagueness of the recommended behaviors. This is, however, a necessary tradeoff given the intent of the theory: to provide guidelines that are appropriate to a wide assortment of situational demands. Accordingly, however, a limitation of any universal approach is that the degree of *fit* to a particular situation will not be as high as a theory that is contingent upon the situation. This limitation has prompted the development of *contingency* theories, which were discussed above.

UNIVERSAL TRAIT LEADERSHIP THEORIES

This approach to leadership argues that individuals with certain traits are more likely to adopt behaviors that are associated with strong leadership, more likely to be perceived as credible, and are accepted by followers. Trait theories help us to understand and distinguish between strong and weak leadership based on the personal traits of the individual leaders. Thus, the focus of this section is to gain an awareness of personal characteristics, which have been found to be important for effective leaders, and this improves our ability to select individuals.

Charismatic Leadership Theory

The charismatic theory argues that there exist universal, personal traits that induce a profound and extraordinary effect on followers. The predominant traits associated with strong charismatic leaders are as follows.

- Strong need for power—Leaders have high self-confidence and a willingness to accept the burdens of responsibility; they also actively build a following by engaging in impression management.
- High need for influence—Leaders derive personal satisfaction from motivating others; they are adept at gaining follower commitment by communicating a positive vision, which defines tasks in terms of ideological goals, holds high expectations of subordinates, and shows confidence in their abilities.
- Job involvement—People with leadership capabilities hold a positive view of the organization, derive personal satisfaction from the job itself, and are active in and committed to the organization.
- Moral righteousness—Leaders demonstrate strong convictions and set the example for subordinates to follow.

The biggest problem with these trait theories has been in determining whether individuals have these characteristics because they are leaders, or whether people developing into leaders acquire these traits. In other words, we are faced with the classic *chicken and egg* question in trait theory: What leads to what? Because these attributes have been drawn from the study of an array of exceptional leaders of the past, these attributes may represent the outcome of a lifetime of effective leadership-building efforts on behalf of the leaders and their organizations rather than representing the cause of effective leadership. Thus, if we do not feel that these leadership attributes currently apply to ourselves, we should not be discouraged from pursuing our own leadership development.

Transformational Leadership Theory

A subset of charismatic leaders, *transformational* leaders are individuals who cause positive, substantial changes in organizations. That is, this type of leader creates a nonroutine transformation of the organization by inspiring the team to achieve organization goals that are not overtly in their own self-interest. For example, we most often think of Lee Iacocca as a transformational leader, based on his dramatic success in turning around Chrysler Corporation. The predominant traits associated with the strong transformational leader are as follows.

- Vision—the ability to clearly conceive the future desired state of the project, team, or organization. Chapters 3 and 4 will explain project vision in detail.
- Communication—the ability to effectively convey ideas and plans, typically through a superior command of language skills, including the use of analogy and metaphor.
- Trust—the ability to consistently demonstrate strong moral character and integrity.
- Action—the ability to readily make decisions and accept responsibility, thereby gaining and maintaining forward momentum.

In contrast, as we noted in Chapter 1, *transactional* leadership is a generally weaker form involving routine, dispassionate interactions with team members, enforcing rules, rewards, sanctions, and so forth. Transactional leaders deal with subordinates based on discrete *transactions:* a subordinate has a question to which the leader responds, a subordinate needs disciplining, and so on. The key to transactional leadership lies often in an emphasis on activities over long-term relationships. It is argued that managers demonstrating transactional leadership are acceptable for maintaining status quo but, lacking the traits of the transformational leader, cannot lead a major transformation of the organization.

CONCLUSION

After reviewing these different approaches to the problem of project leadership, two themes emerge as fundamental and critical: 1) The effective leader takes an active concern for the welfare of the team members, and 2) acts to ensure that the goals of the project are achieved as efficiently as possible. All of the approaches discussed above incorporate these themes, but they approach these issues from very different perspectives. The *universal trait approach* identifies personal characteristics that followers attribute to leaders, which can accomplish both themes simultaneously. The *contingent trait approach* provides a means of matching the leader to the situation in order to achieve both themes simultaneously. The *universal behavior approach* makes the most explicit argument that the pursuit of both themes is appropriate in all situations, and the *contingent behavior approach* identifies important situation characteristics and leader discretionary actions, which allow the leader to maximize the simultaneous achievement of both themes. The importance of these two themes leads to the next fundamental issue: balance. How does the leader achieve balance in pursuing these two themes?

Balancing Concern for the Task and for the Project Member: Pareto Optimality

Maximum leader effectiveness occurs when both themes are achieved simultaneously. On this issue, again, each approach makes a different argument for the means of achieving both themes simultaneously, but the common underlying philosophy is captured in the principal of Pareto Optimality. In 1897, Vilfredo Pareto made the argument that the welfare of participants of an economic system is greatest when all of the participants are made as well off as possible, up to the point where no member can be made better off without making another member worse off. The implication is that, when tradeoffs exist, none of the individual participants' welfare is optimized because to do so would require another individual to be worse off. Thus, the optimal balance represents a compromise between the needs of the team and the needs of the task. Leadership, then, is proactively seeking to simultaneously maximize the welfare of all of the stakeholders.

For example, allowing one team member to leave work early is unfair to the other team members who must work longer to make up for the absence. Such a decision would cause resentment, reduce trust, and lower commitment. Alternatively, allowing all of the team members to leave work early places the project behind schedule, hurting the project and the organization. This would cause organizational representatives to feel resentment, lack of trust, and lower commitment to the project team. The Pareto optimal solution is for the leader to learn the time-schedule requirements of the team members and the organization so that the members can complete their work during times that best fit the needs of the individual, the project, and the organization.

We are now in a position to argue that any individual can begin to improve her leadership by taking the following actions, which are necessary to determine a Pareto optimal balance between the needs of the team and the needs of the project.

1. Learn about the team members (concern for people).
   - Assess their abilities.
   - Assess their need for guidance.
   - Help team members develop their skills.
   - Understand their personal requirements and goals.
2. Learn about the project (concern for the task).
   - Assess the skills and abilities required.
   - Assess the resources required.
   - Structure flexibility into the project plan to accommodate unknowns.
   - Assess the resources available from the organization.
   - Assess how the project meets the goals of the organization.
3. Act for the simultaneous welfare of the individuals and the project—Pareto Optimality (be fair, consistent, equitable). This is the most difficult aspect of leadership, and it cannot be achieved without numbers 1 and 2.
   - Develop goals for the project, which meet both the goals of the organization and the goals of the team members.
   - Match the team members' skills to the needs of the project.
   - Match the resources to the needs of the team.
   - Match the rewards to the needs of the individuals.

A final point concerns the issue of *coordination and control*. While the issue of control was emphasized explicitly in only the contingent-trait approach, it is fundamental to effective completion of any project, and, as the leader is responsible for completion, it is critical that our discussion include recommendations as to how coordination and control can be achieved and improved. Control of any task requires four things: 1) a goal, 2) a measure, 3) a comparison of 1 and 2, and 4) a means of effecting change in the system.

Goal. The leader must identify a desired state of the project. The desired state has many labels: goal, objective, standard, and so on.

Measure. The leader must measure the actual state of the project. The assessment of the project's actual state may be objective or subjective, as long as the measure is valid.

Comparison. The leader must be able to compare the actual state of the project with the desired state. The result of this comparison process is knowledge of the direction of progress toward the desired state.

Effect Change. The leader must be able to cause a change in the direction and/or magnitude of effort on the project.

Figure 6.   Control Theory

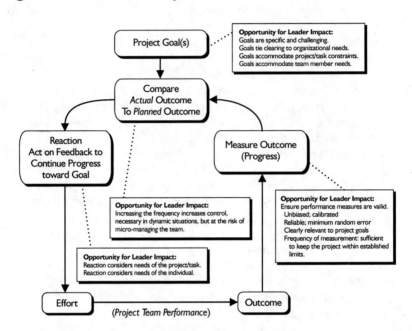

Integrating Leader Concern for People and the Task with Coordination and Control

We can now make recommendations for improving coordination and control to maximize performance of the team and completion of the project. To improve control the leader can perform the following.

■ Clearly articulate the goal: When goals are clear and specific, it is easier to compare the actual performance to desired performance to determine progress. This maximizes potential coordination and control. By articulating how the goal meets the needs of the project, as well as the needs of the team, commitment and trust are enhanced.

■ Use valid measurements: When measures of actual performance are valid, all members have greater trust, commitment, and confidence in the feedback provided from the subsequent comparison to the desired performance. Performance is maximized when the leader selects measures that are acceptable from the perspective of both the project and the team members.

■ Adjust comparison frequency: The leader's control increases as the frequency of the comparison process increases. That is, the greater the frequency of the feedback process, the greater the number of opportunities to take corrective action. However, each comparison process requires new measurement and subsequent action, which is costly in time and resources. Thus, the comparison frequency should be adjusted by the leader to be as low as possible, but still ensure progress toward the goal.

▪ Effect change: Reacting to the feedback, the leader's ability to effect a change in how the project is completed is determined largely by the classical leadership theories that we discussed above. That is, the leader's influence is a function of changing the direction of effort, concern for the task, and increasing motivation—concern for the people.

Any project manager's ability to lead effectively is augmented by his understanding of alternative approaches to leadership. Put another way, it is the rare project leader who successfully operates using one innate leadership style under all circumstances and with all subordinates. Practical realities and a wealth of supporting research demonstrate the opposite effect; strong leaders understand that their own flexibility and willingness to alter their leadership styles to fit the situation and the subordinate are necessary precursors to effective team performance.

This chapter has developed some of the more important leadership models for project managers. As we noted at the beginning of the chapter, *theory* does not have to be a dirty word devoid of any practical implications or managerial usefulness. In fact, an understanding of fundamental leadership theory will make it much easier for novice project managers to learn to recognize their own preferred approaches, analyze situations for appropriate responses, and adjust their styles accordingly.

The key, as we have discussed, is *flexibility*. Flexibility implies a willingness of project leaders to avoid locking themselves into one set leadership style either out of prejudice, laziness, or ignorance. The more we know about leadership behavior, the more we are able to take these alternative styles and add them to our repertoire. Our goal (and the reader's goal, as well) is to develop leadership potential to its maximum. The more we know of alternative leadership approaches, the better prepared we are to do just that.

Accountability for Results

IMAGINE YOURSELF AT a basketball game. There you are seated front-row center when the players take the court. The teams are composed of ten of the finest athletes in the world, and this is championship play. The buzzer sounds, the ball is in the air, and these million-dollar giants take over. The arena is packed, and ten thousand hearts beat as one as twenty thousand eyes follow the ball. Suddenly, a grunt, a flash, and a man is borne into the air. A ball is plunged through a hoop, a glass backboard shatters, and all hell breaks loose. Amidst the hoopla, you glance up to see the score.

But there is no scoreboard! There is nothing but thin air where a scoreboard should be. Suddenly all that was held so closely just seconds before is lost. Despite the wizardry of the athletes and the magic of the moment, the game is nothing without the score.

How many of us have, at one time or another, worked for a manager or project leader who did not keep score? Managers who: 1) could not communicate clear performance expectations; 2) routinely played favorites by holding some team members to one standard and other team members to a different one; 3) offered us no way of tracking or assessing our performance; and 4) evaluated our performance on the project in vague or inconsistent ways?

We suspect that practically every reader will answer "yes" to at least one of the above questions. Few things are more disgruntling in the organizational setting than managers who are incapable of effective accountability. One of the critical behaviors that all effective leaders seem to have in common is their ability to demand high performance expectations and clearly communicate those expectations, while holding all subordinates accountable to the same standards of behavior.

Part of effective leadership is rewarding superior efforts and sanctioning those who shirk. At the front end of many projects, *leaders* will spit bile and pound their chests as though they were silverback gorillas seeking a mate. Yet, come to assessment time and they morph into scampering, tittering rhesus monkeys. The effective leader is one who is adept in granting rewards and sanctions; neither should be excessive. Consistency and fairness in rewards and sanctions build trust and commitment. This is easier said than done; thus, it is helpful to review the process and components of effective versus ineffective accountability systems.

The concept of effective accountability is especially important in project management. Given the constraints of limited time and personnel, this is potentially a *teambuster*, especially so if the home functional units are still part of the accountability system. For team players who feel that they have been cheated, their reactions can be fatal. They may actively rebel, reduce their efforts, sabotage the project, or just take their *ball* and go home.

Accountability, a system of comparing the results achieved by the individual or team to some defined expectation, is *not* a human-resource function. Linking effort and results to consequences is an integral part, not an afterthought, of leadership. The result of this comparison provides a basis for initiating action to reward the superior performer, and sanctioning those who shirk their duties. This chapter provides a brief overview of project leadership processes used to create and, more importantly, ensure such accountability for results. These will be summarized in a generic process model of accountability. We believe that several essential features of any effective accountability system can be derived from an application of this generic model to specific project situations.

FUNCTIONAL ACCOUNTABILITY

Accountability can be harmful as well as helpful. Any level of accountability can be imposed by the leader, due to the leader's formal authority over the project, but not all levels are functional. A level that is too high will cause the team to withdraw from the project; motivation will fall, distrust will develop, and commitment will fall. This occurs because the team is being sanctioned for low performance, which is caused by factors beyond its control. Resentment will ultimately develop. Alternatively, high performers are being rewarded for performance, which, again, is caused by factors beyond the team's control. When this is observed by others, it will be viewed as favoritism, and the high performer may be ostracized. Again, resentment will ultimately develop.

If accountability is too low, motivation will fall as well; good performance is not being recognized, and poor performers are not being corrected. The high performers will observe that there is no penalty imposed on the poor performers, and this, combined with a lack of recognition for their good performance, will cause them to reduce their level of effort to maintain what they perceive to be equity between the work put into the project and the rewards received.

Figure 7.   Accountability Assessment

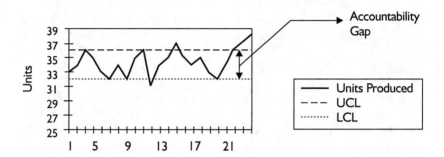

To help illustrate positive from negative accountability structures, we will define the level of accountability in a given situation as the accountability gap, then show how different variables produce levels of accountability that are dysfunctional.

ACCOUNTABILITY GAP

Accountability for performance can be described as the range of performance that goes unrewarded and unsanctioned. That is, accountability is defined by an upper and lower boundary: the closer together these target performance levels are, the higher the level of accountability.

For example, compensation based on commission sales would be considered a high-accountability performance structure: for every sale, the salesperson receives an additional reward (commission), and, for every sale lost, the paycheck is reduced. Since there is no range of performance that goes unrewarded, or sanctioned, accountability is high. Conversely, when there are no levels of performance that earn additional rewards or sanctions, the position has low accountability. For example, a person on salary receives a fixed amount regardless of the actual level of performance. Thus, the accountability gap is wide, and the level of accountability is low.

There are four major features of an accountability system that determine the level of functional accountability: clearly communicating expectations, valid measurement of performance, local control over performance, and timely feedback for corrective action.

COMMUNICATING EXPECTATIONS

That leaders should be effective communicators is common knowledge, but the reasons why are typically less well known. One reason involves accountability. For accountability to be functional, the leader must clearly communicate expectations of performance and consequences of performance. This solves several problems. First, setting goals has been found to have positive motivating effects on subsequent performance. This is especially true when the goals are specific and difficult, yet achievable. When goals are specific, it provides clear direction for effort and increases the team's ability to monitor its progress and stay on track. When goals are difficult, there is a greater sense of pride and satisfaction in successful performance. When the goals are achievable, motivation is high because the team perceives that the accountability system will reward its performance.

Second, the leader must clearly identify the consequences of performance in order to create a sense of equity and motivation. If a reward is announced after successful performance, then two problems develop: 1) The leader has missed an opportunity to use the reward as a motivating mechanism, and, if the idea behind the surprise reward was to create motivation for future projects, then it is wasteful because individuals tend to downplay the desirability of rewards that are not carved in stone; and 2) If other teams are involved, which did not receive equal surprise rewards, then they will suspect favoritism by the leader, and resentment and distrust can develop.

Accountability, then, is limited by the extent to which the leader effectively communicates performance expectations and consequences. That is, functional accountability can only be high when expectations are clearly communicated and understood. This is best achieved when expectations are written. When expectations are in writing, the team has greater confidence that the expectations will not be changed during the project without its knowledge. Unfortunately, it is time consuming, expensive, and difficult to communicate well in writing, especially given that projects often entail many dynamics and unknowns, which are difficult to anticipate prior to the execution of the project. For these reasons, it is common for leaders to communicate expectations verbally and to keep the expectations general and vague, rather than specific. While this may be appropriate, given time and uncertainty factors, it means that high accountability should not be enforced. Thus, the effective leader accommodates this limitation in communicating expectations by widening the gap between performance, which is rewarded and sanctioned. In other words, when we are purposely vague in communicating our expectations, it is important not to be too critically evaluative in sanctioning someone for small differences between their performance and our expectations. Setting the accountability limits/boundaries should be a participative decision. (See the Vroom-Jago Model in Figure 4, for a means of optimizing participation given the situation.) By allowing the team to have input in the accountability process, members will have greater commitment to the project.

Further, it is important that the leader communicate the relevance of the expectations to the needs of the project and organization, as well as demonstrate an awareness of the needs and abilities of the team (as discussed in detail in Chapter 2). That is, the effective leader must do a great deal of homework to determine the needs and constraints of the project, the organization, and the team prior to communicating expectations. Thus, one basic building block of an effective system of accountability is the degree to which project and organizational objectives are explicitly translated into specific operational goals and then effectively communicated to the team.

MEASURING PERFORMANCE

Accountability is only as effective as the performance assessment is valid. When holding the project team accountable for its performance, the leader must take into consideration the accuracy of the performance assessment. If the performance measure is incorrect, the team will be rewarded, or sanctioned, inappropriately. If high accountability is imposed, using an invalid measure of the team's performance, the team will experience high levels of stress. Consequently, the quality of work-life is reduced, and the team's motivation to successfully complete the project is likely to suffer dramatically. To accommodate inaccuracies in the measurement system, the accountability gap is widened. Thus, it is important for the leader to understand the limitations of the performance measure. Measurement error is due to problems of reliability, bias, precision, and relevance.

Measurement Reliability

The problem of reliability involves the extent to which repeated measures of the same item (i.e., performance characteristic) produce exactly the same measurement values. For example, if you step on the bathroom scale, and it reads 185 pounds, and then you immediately step on the scale again, and it reads 188, the next time 184, and so on, the scale is unreliable. To overcome this problem, you could weigh yourself many times and calculate the average. This will closely approximate the true weight if the errors are distributed normally. Thus, the leader should assess the extent to which the performance measure to be adopted is reliable and, if it is not, consider taking repeated measurements in order to calculate the average to be able to approximate the true score.

Measurement Bias

The problem of bias involves the extent to which repeated measures of the same item are incorrect by the same amount, in the same direction. For example, if your true weight is 186 pounds, yet repeated measurements on the scale indicate 188 pounds, then the scale is biased: the error is consistent at plus two pounds. Another example is discrimination, as when a project team leader consistently assesses the performance of men higher than that of women. Clearly then, this is a significant threat to effective accountability and project management. Fundamentally, this is a problem of *calibration*. To overcome this problem, the leader should measure performance, which can be independently verified. If the leader's measurement is consistently different from the independent measurement, and the error is in the same direction, the bias is readily determined. Unfortunately, this is a particularly difficult problem for project leaders, given that many performance measures have no basis for independent verification. The team is likely to comment on this problem when it is perceived. Thus, it is important for the leader to be sensitive to feedback from the team, which indicates that bias is present in the performance measure, and enlarge the accountability gap to accommodate the error while the source of the error is found and corrected.

Measurement Precision

The problem of precision involves the interpretation limits of the scale of measurement. For example, if the scale of measurement is simply *good* or *poor*, we should not rank-order three teams with a rating of *good*, because there is no measurement basis for distinguishing between relative performance within the category. If ranking performance is necessary, the precision of the measure must be increased. This is a problem of imprecision. Conversely, a measure can be overly precise. Consider, for example, measuring the average number of children in a household for a community; typically, the calculated value is something like 2.5743291. This is a very precise measure, but it cannot be correct for any given house since it would require the existence of a fraction of a child. A value of three would be less precise but more valid. Because higher precision is typically achieved at a greater cost to the project, the leader should adopt a scale of measurement with precision that is no greater than necessary for the circumstances. In general, however, the greater the precision of measurement, the higher the level of accountability that can be achieved.

Measurement Relevance

The problem of relevance involves the extent to which the measure captures the intended aspect of performance. Often, the area of performance to be measured is multidimensional and precludes the use of a single measure, or it is abstract and cannot be measured directly. For example, a team's performance expectation is to arrive at work by 8:00 A.M. and leave no later than 5:00 P.M. This expectation is clearly communicated and understood by the team. A time clock is used to measure actual performance, and this measure is valid: the clock is reliable (it keeps time properly), and it is not biased (it has been calibrated, set to the correct time). Further, the time clock records time to the nearest second, which is sufficient precision to determine whether or not a team member is in compliance with expectations. So far, the accountability system will justify a small accountability gap, and therefore a high level of accountability. However, this performance measure does not indicate the type or amount of work actually completed on the project. Thus, the leader and the team may experience dissatisfaction with this accountability system. This dissatisfaction is likely because the aspect of performance held accountable does not capture the quality of the work and offers little meaningful feedback with which to improve the project. Thus, it is important for the project leader to assess and clearly explain the relevance of performance measures to the team or structure team participation in the decision-making process of selection.

CONTROL OVER RESULTS

Accountability systems only work when the team has control over the results. Rewarding and sanctioning serve no purpose if the outcomes are beyond the control of the team. Quite the contrary, holding the team accountable for performance that is beyond its control will produce stress and withdrawal. Thus, the effective leader designs the project in a manner that maximizes the team's control over results. This is achieved by developing knowledge and skills though training, matching team members' abilities to project tasks, and structuring the project to accommodate unforeseeable events.

Knowledge and Skill

The project leader should not expect performance from team members who lack the knowledge required to complete the task successfully. Even if the team member has the knowledge, there may exist a lack of experience, which makes the individual perform more slowly or inefficiently. Thus, it is important that the project leader adjust the accountability gap to account for the current level of knowledge and skill. This, of course, will change over time as both knowledge and skill are developed with training and experience. Therefore, the accountability gap should adjust over time, as well, to reflect the stage of development for each team member. That is, the accountability gap should be initially wide to accommodate the team members' struggle to adjust to the new project task structure and environment. As the team members learn and adapt to the situation, the accountability gap should narrow. As mentioned previously, changes in the accountability gap should include the participation of the team members to ensure feelings of equity and to build commitment and trust. The type and extent of participation by the team in the decision process should depend on the situation (see the Vroom-Jago Model discussion in Chapter 2).

External Influences

Most projects involve significant uncertainties and dynamic complexities, which cannot be eliminated from the project completely; thus, the degree of control achieved by the team is seldom complete, nor is it zero. Accordingly, the project leader should not hold the team accountable for performance that results from unpredictable external events. To maximize accountability, the leader should structure the project to minimize the influence of the external events. This may be achieved through buffering, leveling, rationing, and delegating.

Buffering. Buffering project performance from external events typically involves structuring slack resources into the project. For example, if a task requires eight days to complete, the schedule might be structured to allow ten days. Accordingly, a higher level of accountability can be imposed on performance.

Leveling. Unforeseen events can result in greater demands on a team than anticipated in the project plan. If this causes the team to *rush* its work to keep up, a low-quality output is expected. Thus, it is the job of the leader to structure flexibility into the schedule, to smooth out or level the demands placed on the team, so that it can perform efficiently and effectively. By leveling the demands on the team, a higher level of accountability can be successfully achieved.

Rationing. External events can cause the requirements of the project to increase. When this change overwhelms the buffering and leveling options available, the project leader must make the difficult decision of how to scale back the size or scope of the project to meet the resources and capabilities of the team. If this is not possible, the leader must ration the team's efforts on the various aspects of the project. This rationing will change the performance expected of the team, and the leader should adjust the accountability gap to accommodate the new requirements on the team. Thus, rationing should be avoided and used only when buffering and leveling are insufficient to accommodate the external impacts on the team's performance.

Delegating. Often, external changes can be accommodated immediately by the team members if they have the authority to adjust the structure of their tasks. This authority must be clearly delegated by the project leader in order to instill confidence and trust. This is a delicate problem because if too much control over the tasks is delegated, then coordination of effort between team members is destroyed. Thus, the leader should delegate as much control over the work as possible, up to the point when changes made by one team member will materially affect the performance of another. Thus, when delegating, the project leader must establish clear boundaries, or *set fences*, around the domain within which the team members may freely make changes. In general, the greater the authority delegated to the team, the greater the control the team has over its performance, the greater the environmental events that can be accommodated, and, thus, the greater the level of accountability that can be achieved.

Output versus Behavior Control

When external events have a large effect on the team's level of control over project outcomes, or when the outcomes are abstract and difficult to measure with satisfactory validity, the project leader has the option of switching from outcome-based performance to behavior-based performance. In this case, the accountability system is based on expectations and measures of team behaviors, which cause the outcomes. The idea is that the team has more control over its behavior than it has over the consequences of that behavior. This is the better option when there exists a proven, optimal way of conducting the work. The disadvantage of behavior-based accountability systems is the lack of flexibility and discretion available to the team members in conducting their work. This lack of autonomy can reduce the internal satisfaction that the team members experience on the project, resulting in a lower level of motivation. Further, since outcomes are not part of the accountability system, it is more difficult to keep the project on the timeline. Overall, then, the project leader may consider using a combination of outcome-based and behavior-based performance measures to exploit the benefits of each.

Identifiability

A final issue concerns identifiability and shared responsibility. Accountability systems are only appropriate when the team, or team member, is clearly identified with the performance. When individual contribution to performance is clearly identifiable, then accountability at the individual level is appropriate and effective. However, tasks may require the interdependent contributions of several individuals. In this case, individual contribution is difficult to distinguish from the group's performance. In such a case, accountability at the individual level is destructive since rewards and sanctions are driven by performance of other team members, which is beyond the control of the individual member. Accountability can be achieved, however, by measuring the performance of the group, or team, rather than of the individual. That is, as a group, the team has control over its performance, so accountability at that level is functional. In general, as identifiability with performance increases, higher accountability can be achieved.

FEEDBACK AND REACTION TO RESULTS

Having established and communicated expectations to the team, having structured the work to maximize the team's control over its performance, and having established and taken measures of team performance, accountability then becomes a function of comparing actual results to the expectations. The result of this comparison process is the determination of whether the team's performance meets or exceeds the expectations. This is the basis of feedback to the project leader and the team. While it is important that the leader conduct the comparison process to invoke the accountability system, it is also helpful to provide the team with the capability to measure its own performance so that it can conduct the comparison and generate the feedback for itself. This *self-management* allows the team to make adjustments without the intervention of the leader in order to meet and exceed expectations. (This assumes that the project leader has delegated authority to make changes). This reduces the demands on the project leader, and the autonomy afforded the team can increase members' intrinsic satisfaction from the work, resulting in increased motivation and improved performance. The tradeoff is the lack of accountability; the leader is not rewarding or sanctioning. Thus, it is always necessary for the project leader to periodically compare actual performance to expectations and provide feedback to the team.

The frequency of the feedback process has a large impact on the effectiveness of the accountability system. In general, the higher the frequency of the comparison process, the better the feedback to the team. That is, the leader and the team can only make informed decisions on how to proceed when feedback is available. The higher the frequency, the greater the number of opportunities to make changes and check the results of previous changes. It is also true, however, that the higher the frequency, the higher the cost of the accountability system. Each comparison process consumes time and resources.

To optimize the tradeoff between the benefits and costs of generating feedback, the project leader should assess the dynamics of the project environment in terms of how quickly the team's performance can break the accountability boundaries. Highly dynamic environments justify the costs of frequent feedback because the team has a greater number of opportunities to make changes. Conversely, frequent feedback in stable environments can be considered an annoyance by the team, as the comparison process will not provide information that is substantial enough to justify taking time to absorb it. This is sometimes referred to as *micro-management*. This can be avoided by reducing the frequency and by providing the means of *self-management* feedback, as discussed above, which allows the team to absorb feedback at its own pace.

If the results consistently fail to meet expectations, some form of corrective action needs to be considered. Before taking action, however, the organization must first consider whether the expectations should be changed because they are unrealistically high, or whether there are environmental constraints on the entity that preclude the team from being able to achieve the current expectations. If neither of these is responsible for the lack of results, then corrective action must be implemented.

Corrective Action

A corrective action is any event that produces a change in performance. The resulting change in results is limited by the degree to which the project leader and the team have control over performance. Further, because tradeoffs exist, changes may improve some aspects of performance and reduce others. To document the success of the change, the results should be remeasured in a subsequent period. The frequency of measurement should temporarily increase until an appropriate corrective action is found and performance is determined to meet expectations.

Corrective action is initiated by the detection of a discrepancy between the desired and actual state of performance, as discussed above, but this discrepancy is driven fundamentally by a lack of knowledge or lack of motivation. The accountability boundaries address the latter; the accountability gap accommodates the former.

When performance falls short of expectations, it may be the result of a lack of knowledge of the internal processes (abilities, resources required, and so on) or external events or both. That is, projects are seldom conducted under conditions of complete certainty. As such, progress on these projects is made via conjectures and refutations or trial and error: the team tries an approach and absorbs the feedback as either a rejection of that approach or a confirmation. Indeed, the success of one of America's most famous and formidable projects, The Manhattan Project (the building of the atomic bomb), was attributed to trial and error by physicist John Wheeler, who stated: "The whole idea was to make mistakes as fast as possible."

The accountability system is not intended to react to feedback generated as a means of acquiring knowledge. This is why the accountability gap exists. A certain range of performance variation is functional in that it allows the team to learn and take risks without fear of reprisal. However, past a certain point, it becomes clear that poor performance is due to a lack of effort, or shirking, and accountability must be invoked. Failure to hold such performance accountable will produce feelings of inequity in the team members who are not shirking. Correspondingly, superior performance should be acknowledged, as well, to maintain feelings of equity in that superior effort will be rewarded.

A PROCESS MODEL OF ACCOUNTABILITY

The model presented in Figure 8 summarizes and illustrates the relationships that have been highlighted in this overview. As summarized in the model, the project leader's ability to enhance desired results can be facilitated by:

- explicitly defining and communicating expectations
- increasing the validity of the measures used to evaluate performance
- increasing the team's control over its performance
- providing meaningful incentives for motivating high performance
- adjusting the frequency of measuring and evaluating results to fit the dynamics of the situation
- providing timely and specific feedback to the team about its results
- initiating corrective action based on the feedback.

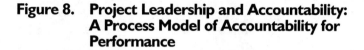

Figure 8. Project Leadership and Accountability: A Process Model of Accountability for Performance

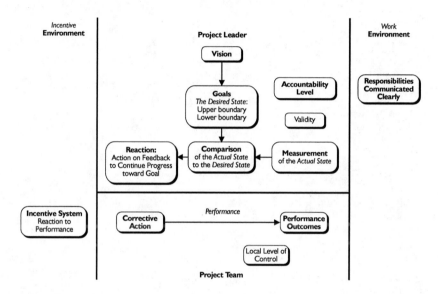

As each of these factors is improved, the accountability gap may be narrowed, increasing the level of accountability for that aspect of performance, which maximizes both performance and the satisfaction experienced by the team. When these accountability factors can no longer be improved, it is the task of the leader to assess the situation and adjust the accountability gap to accommodate lack of control, measurement problems, unclear expectations, and infrequent or poor quality feedback. Structuring participation and self-management into the accountability system will help to optimize its effectiveness.

CHAPTER 4

Creating a Project Vision: The Image That Guides the Team's Work

VISION IS A loaded word. Ask ten people on the street to define it, and you will probably receive ten different definitions. Ask the street preacher, and he may cite visions of imminent celestial arrivals, repentance, and heavenly glory. Ask the politician, and she will go on and on about her vision of tomorrow, which, if not implemented, will only result in a continued societal slide toward hell on earth. Vision, as a word, has always had dual implications: that of illusion, and that of foresight. It is a word that can be used with ease by madmen and wise men alike.

As a result, it is easy to see why many managers are made uncomfortable by the word. Yet if asked what single trait is essential for effective leadership, most would simply reply, "Vision." This entire concept can be especially difficult for the project manager to accept. Most project managers are characterized and rewarded as *can-do* sorts of people who keep their feet firmly planted on the ground—no head-in-the-clouds attitudes here. For many project managers, especially those with strong technical skills, the idea of vision may seem not only ridiculous but also potentially dangerous, and many will strongly oppose it. Yet, vision is an essential component of transformational leadership, strongly associated with innovative change. The ability of a project manager to visualize and communicate a project's aims, methodology, and definition of success is paramount for effective leadership.

Yet vision is more than just merely a planning tool. The essence of vision is the transfer of values of the leader to the organization. *What is important? Why is it important? Why should others care about the importance?* A manager will use vision to demonstrate his ideas of the future and the potential benefits for those who follow. Visioning is an important part of creating effective relationships between leaders and followers that can mean the difference between project success and failure.

A great deal of research evidence exists that demonstrates the value of a well-articulated vision. This evidence suggests that organizational transformations and innovations are more successful when the leader has communicated an organizational vision. In addition, followers appear to be more loyal and committed to their organizations, trust corporate leadership more, take more pride in their organizations, and are more satisfied with their jobs when the leader has provided a vision. Recent studies even suggest that a well-defined corporate vision will positively impact an organization's bottom line. Leadership vision is associated with more successful leaders and companies.

Despite the evidence that organizational visions can make a difference, they have also gotten some bad press recently, particularly from a well-known comic strip character who mocks business leaders. The problem with the concept of vision, however, is real and has resulted from misconceptions about what an organizational vision is, and how it should be developed and used by leaders. The first part of the problem is the belief by some that vision is a mystical concept—like using a crystal ball or waving a wand over followers to make them do extraordinary things. This discourages some business leaders from trying to utilize the concept. In practice, an organizational vision is much less magical. A vision is simply a positive image of the future that a leader has or develops and then communicates to followers. A basic feedback model can be used to explain how the vision then produces the desired outcomes.

A second part of the problem relates to the method used by many leaders to develop an organizational vision. Some leaders write brief statements, often while on a retreat with executives, and call the statements *organizational visions*. Typically, these vision statements are written to please board members, stockholders, and the public. It is often difficult to tell one organization's vision statement from another's. These statements are meant to summarize everything that the organization stands for and is trying to achieve. They may or may not be internalized by the leaders, have the leaders' commitment, or provide any concrete direction for followers. It is unlikely that these types of vision statements will have any positive impact on the organization, but it is very likely that followers will know that. This chapter will describe the potential impact and theory behind well-developed and clearly communicated project visions. The next chapter will present an approach to developing a project vision, which can produce the desired results.

THE MOTIVATIONAL IMPACT OF A VISION

A number of experts on leadership have speculated about how vision works and why it appears to have the impact that it does. The conclusion that most have reached is that a vision motivates followers whose behavior and work performance changes and improves. This motivation occurs because the vision inspires and energizes followers, creates a bridge to the future, provides direction, establishes a standard, and motivates leaders, as well.

Inspires and Energizes Followers

The vision presents a picture of a positive outcome for the project and the project team. An effective vision is positive, even idealistic. It presents an image of a near-perfect world, identifying what is possible if the team members pull together and work hard. Typically, the person who communicates the vision is someone who is also very positive and optimistic about the project. The positive image and upbeat delivery are inspiring and make people feel good. Research has shown that not all people are positive about their lives. When followers are negative, they do not perform as well; but when followers feel optimistic, it energizes them. If a team is facing a new project, it is particularly important to give the members an extra shot of energy. Beginning a challenging project can be overwhelming. However, when a project leader provides the vision of a positive outcome for the organization, the team, and each individual, followers are more likely to start the new project on a *high*—which can be critical to the project's success. A vision also creates meaning for followers. It helps them understand, or *see*, how they, as individuals, fit into the big picture, and this has a motivating effect, as well.

Creates a Bridge to the Future

Hope for the future is what motivates most people, whether it is for the day ahead to go better than the day before, that next year they will be working on a job that they love, or that five years from now their companies will be successful and growing. Positive feelings about the future get people out of bed earlier and working harder. However, many people are not future oriented. For a variety of reasons, including individual personality characteristics, culture, and life situations, many people are oriented toward the past or the present. It is the leader's responsibility to pull followers into the future, to see where the organization, or team, is headed. A vision creates that bridge. It shows the followers what the future holds and makes it look positive. Project team members may be exhausted from the work on a previous project, or they may be focused on barriers that they face on a new project, or they may have personal problems that interfere with their ability to focus on the future. For these and other reasons, the future may seem far away and unimportant. The vision is the tool that the leader can use to pull followers into the future.

Provides Direction

A well-defined and articulated vision tells followers where the organization is headed. It provides a road map, so to speak, of the direction for the future. This allows followers to understand how to adjust their own work so that it is consistent with the organization's goals. The vision may also help the follower understand whether personal goals are consistent with organizational goals. If not, that follower may need to change organizations. For example, if a project team is developing and launching a new product that requires the use of a specific technology of little interest to a project team member, that member will have to decide whether to develop the expertise required or leave that team. Although this idea may seem simplistic, it is very common in organizational settings for people to be so caught up in day-to-day tasks that they lose sight of the goals of the organization, not to mention personal goals. The vision brings gaps between personal goals and organizational goals into focus for both leaders and followers.

Establishes a Standard

An effective vision is challenging. Because a vision is written to be idealistic, it provides a standard to which followers can aspire but not easily or quickly attain. Research on goal setting suggests that challenging objectives lead to significantly higher performance than when easy goals are set or when followers are simply told to "do their best." When a project manager outlines a vision for a project, a standard is established, which should lead to a higher level of performance than when no vision is available to followers.

Motivates Leaders

A vision also affects the motivation of the leader. A vision is the deal between the leader, the followers, and the organization. Once the leader has communicated the vision publicly, it becomes a contractual obligation. Research suggests that when commitments are public, people are more likely to strive to keep them. Psychologically, the leader feels compelled to attain the vision and, as a result, may spend more time and energy to fulfill the obligation.

Developing a vision also provides the leader with the opportunity to think strategically before planning. Developing the vision over a period of a few weeks allows the human mind an incubation period, which will open up more opportunities and creative solutions to project barriers. It has been suggested that too often leaders develop the plan before they develop the vision. Premature planning can limit the scope and potential outcomes of a project. For example, it would be common to find project leaders who are given projects and immediately begin detailed planning to complete the projects, as assigned, without thinking about additional potential outcomes for users and the organization, creative approaches to solving problems and getting around barriers, and best-case scenarios. The time spent developing and communicating a positive vision can lead to different paradigms and better results in the long run.

EXPLAINING HOW VISION WORKS

A simple feedback model explains how visions works (see Figure 9). A vision is a mental image that exists in the mind of the leader. If the leader is committed to the vision, behaves in a manner consistent with the vision, and communicates the vision well, followers will have a clear standard with which to compare their behavior. This suggests that a vision acts as a metagoal; it sits at the top of a hierarchy of lower-level goals (Thoms and Govekar In Press). The vision answers the question: "Why am I doing this?" Lower-level goals answer the question: "What do I need to do to accomplish the vision?" Once the vision is clearly articulated, the lower-level goals, project steps, and planning can begin. It is important to note that project managers will have visions for the projects that they are leading, which may actually be lower-level goals at the organizational level.

On project teams, a shared vision may be more appropriate than a leader vision. A leader vision is a vision developed and driven by one leader, typically the person with the most legitimate or power position in an organization. Shared vision refers to a vision developed and driven by a group of people who have similar levels of power or influence, due to either their positions or their expertise, and respect of other members of the group. Project leaders may want to involve team members in the development of the vision because of varying types and levels of expertise found on project teams. Technically, it would be impossible for a group of individuals to have identical mental images of the future. However, if individuals take the time to develop a vision together, they can enjoy

Figure 9.   A Control Theory Model of Organizational Vision

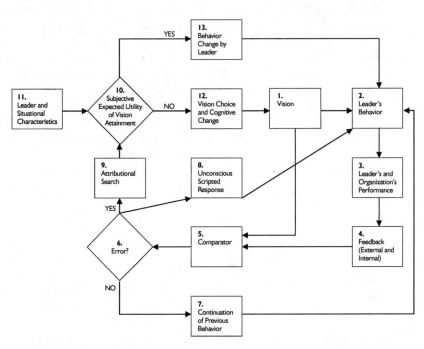

some of the same benefits of a vision developed and driven by a single leader. Throughout the rest of this chapter, and in the next, the differences between the effects of leader and shared vision will be explained.

The Vision Is the Standard

The vision serves as the standard in the model, similar to the temperature setting on a thermostat. It directs behavior and serves as the referent for performance. The leader—or team, in the case of a shared vision—attempts to behave or perform in ways consistent with the vision.

Behavioral Responses to the Vision

The most important behavior of a leader is the selection of team members. The vision will guide the choice of people and decisions regarding the technical expertise needed for the team. For example, if a project leader chooses the team members before developing the project vision, key specialties may be overlooked, and the original team may be incapable of fulfilling the vision developed later. Adding and eliminating team members is more difficult after the project begins than it is before it begins.

A second behavioral response to a vision is strategic planning. A team will typically spend many hours planning the approach to a new project. When the team has a well-defined vision, this planning process can be targeted and streamlined. The plan tells the leader and the team exactly how the vision will be accomplished. It lays out the various steps that will be followed, who will complete each stage, and precisely what the performance expectations are.

Another behavioral response is the communication of the vision. The vision must be communicated to all followers, team members, and constituents. A project leader who is committed to a project vision will be particularly diligent about articulating and explaining the project to all organizational members who have a stake in or impact on the project's success. This assures the project leader that the vision meets the needs of constituents, and it is also a way of eliciting necessary support. In the cases when a vision is developed by a project team, communication is the primary method used to make sure that the mental image that one team member has is consistent with the vision of colleagues. The more the leader and the team talk about the vision, the better the chances are that it will be achieved.

A fourth behavioral response to a vision is the choice of tasks, the scheduling of the tasks, and the amount of effort that will be expended on the tasks. The vision should clearly indicate how the leader and team members should be spending their time. For example, if the project leader must decide whether to put more effort into the market research or the technical development of a new product project, the vision should provide the answer. Suppose that the vision suggests that this product design is technology driven and that long-term sales will come from future versions. In this situation, the technical aspects should be the focus, and market research can be put in a secondary position. Another example would be if a member of a project team were trying to decide whether to begin designing the spreadsheet before talking with the project customers or to interview the end users of the project first; the vision should provide the answer. If the vision emphasizes a strong consumer orientation, the team member will know that it is important to interview the customer first. In both of these examples, it is clear that without the vision, the acceptable behavior is either open to the individual's discretion or requires direction from the leader. With the vision, the individual knows how to behave.

Another extremely important behavioral response to a vision by a leader is modeling the behavior that is desired. If accomplishing the vision requires working weekends, the leader must work weekends. If a project leader wants extensive communication with end users during project development, the leader must maintain a continuous dialogue with stakeholders. In the case of shared vision, the team leaders will model the behavior that they expect from their colleagues. Keeping in mind that it would be impossible for a group of people to have an identical mental image of how a project will look when completed, modeling the behavior that members expect of the team is one of the ways that leaders make sure that team members are *on the same page.*

Feedback

Successful project teams need methods for evaluating project task performance and for providing feedback. On any project, feedback is a critical component. Feedback tells the leader and team members whether behavioral responses are correct and consistent with the vision. For example, a team member might be told by the leader that she did not complete enough work and that if she does not increase her work speed, the project will fall short of the envisioned time schedule. The leader should frame feedback in the context of the vision in order to help the follower make necessary comparisons between current performance and the performance required to achieve the vision—in other words: "Your performance is in line with the vision" or "Your performance is not sufficient to lead to accomplishment of a certain aspect of the vision." Feedback should be given frequently by the project leader and should contain specific information.

Comparison Process

It has been said that the difference between managers and leaders is that managers do things right, and leaders do the right things (Bennis and Nanus 1985). It is critical for project leaders to know that the tasks that are important to the accomplishment of the vision are the tasks that are being performed. Feedback can be used by the leader and team members to compare and determine whether they are doing the right things and making the progress necessary to achieve the vision. The more frequent the feedback, the more often followers will compare their performance against the standard. This comparison process may be done subconsciously or consciously. Humans are continuously subconsciously monitoring information for consistency with past experience and their goals.

Whenever they find that there is an error during this comparison process, they must respond if the gap is important. People also consciously review their behavior, especially when a problem occurs, in order to resolve problems or to set new directions for their lives or simply the work aspects of their lives.

There are three possible outcomes of the comparison process.

1. The behavior necessary to accomplish the vision is not being done—an error exists.

2. The behavior necessary to accomplish the vision is on target, and there are no errors or gaps between expectations and performance.

3. The behavior necessary to accomplish the vision is more than is expected, or it is exceeding requirements necessary to achieve the vision. If the behavior is on target or exceeding what is necessary to accomplish the vision, no corrections are needed. However, when the leader or a team member finds an error, changes are necessary.

Errors

Most people respond to errors without thinking much about them. For example, suppose that a leader discovers that some technical aspect of a project is not being addressed appropriately. The leader simply calls the team member with the expertise and asks that individual to look into the situation. Project leaders make routine adjustments like this all the time.

However, if the leader contacts the technical expert and is told that the individual cannot handle the problem because he does not have the specific skills required, the leader has to deliberately process this error. The first step is trying to determine why the error occurred. Using what is called an attributional search, the project leader needs to think about whether she chose the right person for the team, or whether the vision was communicated clearly, or if a new problem, that could not have been anticipated, occurred. The leader may need to determine who is at fault. Then, the second step is for the leader to determine the expected value of vision attainment. In other words, the project leader must decide if it is worthwhile to make the behavioral and cognitive changes necessary to achieve the vision. Conscious processing of errors also involves characteristics of both the leader and the situation. The leader who is not committed to an organization or is upset with senior management may decide to revise the vision. If the organization is being purchased by a group of executives, including the project leader, the leader may decide to do whatever is necessary to make the vision a reality.

Behavior and Cognitive Changes, or Revising the Vision

Humans are constantly reviewing their goals and recommitting or discarding them. When people take responsibility for an error, there are a number of possible responses ranging from changing and improving performance to resignation. If a leader or team member is committed to the vision and feels capable of changing his behavior, the individual will adjust his performance level and attempt to correct the error.

In the case of a project vision, the leader must decide whether the vision should be revised or maintained whenever a difficult error occurs. Due to the public nature of visions, they are harder to discard than personal goals. The project leader—or team members, in the case of a shared vision—will usually decide to keep the vision intact and find the solution to the problem. This may involve hiring a new team member and incurring additional expense to make the vision a reality. If hiring a new team member will put the project over budget, and a goal is to come in under budget, the error will be a bit more complicated to resolve and require additional conscious processing. If a leader is not capable of performing up to the level of the vision, he may get more training, try to transfer off the team, or even leave the organization.

Project leaders must be particularly diligent during the comparison process and help both themselves and team members find acceptable ways of changing their behavior so that it is consistent with the vision. If errors are occurring due to system problems, the leader may need to run interference for team members. If errors are occurring because team members do not understand the vision or the standards, the leader must reinforce or reexplain the vision and the lower-level goals. This could also indicate that the vision is not vivid enough; i.e., it does not provide enough detailed information. If a team member does not have the necessary skills, the team leader must provide development opportunities or decide whether to replace that individual on the project. As much as a project leader may hate it when an error occurs, errors provide extremely valuable information about whether the team is on target to achieve the vision. The errors allow both the leader and the team members to adjust their behavior and thinking, enhancing the potential for success.

IMPLICATIONS FOR PROJECT LEADERS

The feedback model explains how an effectively developed and communicated vision works and provides guidance for project leaders who want to improve their teams' projects. A number of tips for project leaders regarding the use of an organizational vision can be derived from this model.

Project leaders must develop and communicate a positive and future-oriented vision for each project. The research is in. Organizational visions work when they are used appropriately.

Project leaders should be chosen based on their leadership ability, as well as for their technical expertise. Leaders who are naturally positive and future oriented can easily develop and communicate an effective vision. Most likely, these are the kind of people who are promoted to leadership positions. However, project teams are frequently headed by people who are chosen for their technical expertise rather than for their leadership abilities. There are a number of ways to determine whether a potential project manager has the ability to develop a positive project vision, one of which would be to listen to the person talk. Does she talk about the future, how she *sees* the project developing, what she would like to accomplish in the future? Does she use a positive approach when asked how she would deal with hypothetical situations? These are the types of things that you should hear if someone has the ability to lead a project team. In addition, look at the potential project manager's previous project work. Did she use a positive future-oriented approach on previous work? Was she open to new ideas instead of depending on established practices and approaches? Negative and/or past-oriented people can play a useful role on project teams, but *leader* is not one of them.

A project vision should be vivid or elaborate enough that it can provide direction and information to the leader and, when well communicated, to followers. This means that a statement or a paragraph of intent is not a vision. Although this statement might serve a political purpose, it will not do the same job that a well-defined vision will do. A vision will be a complex mental image that includes all aspects of the project. It may at some point be put in written form, but it should be very long and detailed.

The project leader should communicate the vision publicly. This will accomplish two purposes. First, by talking about the vision, the leader creates the contract between himself and the organization and makes a public commitment to accomplish the vision. Second, communicating the vision provides direction and information necessary for team members in order to behave in ways consistent with the vision.

Once the vision is developed and articulated, the leader must behave in ways consistent with the vision. This includes deciding how to spend her time, choosing team members who are likely to perform and deliver the needed skills, developing a strategic plan that will eventually lead to accomplishment of the vision, modeling the type of behavior that she wants from the team, and continuously communicating the vision to team members and other constituents.

The leader and team members have to remember that a vision is a cognitive image, which is difficult to communicate. The leader may have a clear positive image of what the project should look like, but it will be very difficult to completely communicate that image. That is why it is critical for the leader to communicate the vision in a variety of ways: verbally, in writing, and by setting an example.

The project leader must constantly seek and provide feedback regarding the performance of the team. The leader needs feedback on his own behavior and performance as it relates specifically to the vision. A system of checks should be built into the planning process that will provide the leader and the team members with adequate information to detect errors.

The project leader should design opportunities for team members to compare their performance with the vision. Many people avoid comparisons with standards because they do not want bad news. The leader must not only provide feedback but also encourage followers to make comparisons with the standards identified by the vision.

The project leader should seek errors and treat them as learning experiences. After the comparison process is done, the project leader needs to identify the gaps between both her own and the team's behavior and the vision, and find ways to bridge them. This is one of the most important uses of a vision. It provides a method for leaders to ensure that they are doing the right things. For example, assume that an important part of a project leader's vision is the total satisfaction of the project's customer. The project manager builds a system for checking customer perceptions at regular intervals. During one of these checks, the leader discovers that the customer is concerned about the amount of time that the project is taking. This is an error. Without a vision, this customer's concern may not even be considered an error. The leader must now decide either to adjust the vision or find a way to maintain the standard of total satisfaction despite the customer's current concerns regarding time of completion.

It is the job of the leader to make sure that the vision is retained and that the team finds a way to correct errors. The leader must maintain the vision—keep the standards high. In the example given above, the temptation of many team members may be to placate the customer with excuses or provide a rationale as to why the original standard was *unrealistic*. The leader has to refuse to buy the excuses and drive the team forward, exploring alternatives to keep the customer satisfied. This may require adding additional work hours. It may require changing software. It may require taking a shortcut on some other aspect of the project.

CONCLUSION

The purpose of this chapter has been to point out the value of organizational vision. Vision is a useful concept, which has been validated by research. Despite the value that it adds to organizational performance, it is often overlooked or misunderstood and misused by leaders. It appears that an effective vision can improve the chances for successful innovations and transformations, improve team members' morale and commitment to the organization, and impact the bottom line. This chapter explained how vision works using a simple feedback model with vision as the standard or metagoal at the top of other organizational or project goals. This chapter also outlined practical implications of this model for project managers. Developing and effectively communicating a project vision may be the most effective tool that a project leader can use.

CHAPTER 5

Developing a Project Vision: A Step-by-Step Approach

MANY PEOPLE WONDER where great leaders get their visions. Are they born with the ability to create a vision of the future? Are they taught to create a vision in their business school courses or training classes? The answer to both questions is "yes." Some recent research suggests that some leaders seem more capable than others of creating a positive image of the future (Thoms 1994). And, some leaders are being taught specific techniques that can be used to develop organizational visions. This chapter will briefly explore both questions and then present an approach that can be used by managers to develop project visions. The chapter will distinguish between project visions developed by a project leader and shared project visions developed by a team, and explain when each approach is better. The chapter will conclude with tips on communicating the vision.

VISIONARY LEADERS: BORN OR MADE?

It appears that there are certain individual characteristics that make some people better at creating an organizational vision than others are. Three characteristics that have been discussed in the leadership literature are a positive attitude toward life, a future orientation, and creativity. Although there are probably more individual differences that affect vision development, these are the ones that are most often discussed by leadership experts.

A Positive Attitude toward Life

Research suggests that some people are more positive than others (Thoms 1994). They have better outlooks on life, and this affects the way that they think about their organizations and the future. Intuitively, it makes sense that if individuals feel positive about life, they will be more likely to think about their organizations or new project assignments in an optimistic way. Other people are negative in their outlooks on life and that is also reflected in the way that those individuals think about their organizations and their work.

There are a number of ideas about what makes one person more optimistic or positive than another. Part of the explanation is due to innate personality differences between people. Even siblings raised in the same home often differ in their attitudes about life. Yet, the way and the culture in which people are raised will also affect their positivism. In addition, some believe that our attitudes are shaped by the situations in which we find ourselves. For example, we would expect people living in poverty who have little control over their lives to be less optimistic than people who have sufficient money and education and many choices about the way they live. Whatever the cause of a positive attitude toward life, recent research has shown that those people who are positive are better able to create positive images of the future.

Future Orientation

Research also shows that some people are more future oriented than others are (Thoms 1994). It appears that some humans tend to focus on the past, while others focus on the present, and still others, on the future. This focus may manifest itself in the ways that people think about themselves. For example, some people picture themselves in the past, reliving good experiences or trying to change past behavior. Another manifestation of this time orientation may be in the amount of time and energy that is devoted to preparing and planning for the future. For example, some people never think about the future, save for the future, or think about how they will live or what they will be doing in the future. Others may make elaborate plans and begin doing things today that will benefit themselves in twenty years. Again, the reasons why some people are more future oriented than others are complex and probably range from innate differences to cultural and situational reasons. Recent research has shown that leaders who are more future oriented are better able to create an organizational vision (Thoms 1994).

There is also a great deal of creativity involved in developing an organizational vision. An effective vision presents new possibilities, explores alternative paradigms, looks beyond current trends, and ignores traditional barriers. It is commonly accepted that some people are more creative than others. Although many people believe that visionary leaders have unique creative powers, characterized as mystical or magical in some cases, many effective leaders use special techniques, much like artists do, to generate creative ideas. These techniques may have been learned from their parents, teachers, professors, trainers, or from books that they have read. Whatever the source of the creativity, it does appear that creative leaders are better able to develop and utilize organizational visions than those who are not creative.

Based on this evidence, and the probability that there are additional characteristics that make some individuals better at creating positive images of the future, it is clear that some people are *natural* leaders. They may not need any training or encouragement and are likely to be creating positive images of the future in their minds on an ongoing basis. These images drive their day-to-day behavior, which then inspires others to adjust their own thinking and behavior. These leaders, people like Bill Gates and Mahatma Gandhi, frequently begin and lead successful organizations and societal movements, and they often make significant changes in their communities and the world. The rest of the population recognizes these visionary leaders and will follow them. However, not everyone has this gift, and most people need some help developing the images that will allow them to make transformational changes in their organizations.

VISION TRAINING

Most visionary leaders probably develop and maintain positive images of the future continuously and have been doing so for most of their lives. A variety of vision training books and programs exist to help leaders develop visions. These materials and programs typically take one of two approaches: the strategic planning approach, or the creativity approach.

The Strategic Planning Approach

Books and training programs that use the strategic planning approach walk leaders through a series of steps that resemble a strategic planning exercise. For example, one such book asks leaders to do a number of things, including the following (Nanus 1992).

■ Consider the business that they are in and how they operate.
■ Consider their constituencies.

■ Identify current industry trends.
■ Develop alternative scenarios for the future.
■ Choose the *right* vision.

This approach to vision training is also found in many programs offered by a number of large consulting organizations. One advantage to this approach is that it leads to a tangible product—the vision can be developed using familiar and concrete steps. The vision will be realistic, something the authors think is important. One concern with this type of vision training is the fact that it merges visioning with strategic planning. In the last chapter, it was suggested that visioning should precede the planning process. A project vision should not be limited by trends, organizational conditions, and barriers and limitations. The vision should be an idealistic, not a realistic, and challenging image of the future, not an image that has taken into account all of the limitations. This approach infers that we can and should try to predict the future and that this prediction must drive our project. A vision is not a prediction. A vision is an image of the best possible outcomes, which we want to achieve—in spite of the trends, barriers, and limitations.

A second problem with this approach is that it often focuses more on the communication of the vision rather than on the development of the image. Although it is critical that a leader know how to communicate a vision to followers, the vision must first be articulated in the mind of the leader. After the image is formed, communication of the vision will evolve naturally and will take a variety of forms, including changing and modeling appropriate behavior, as well as talking with followers. Ask any corporate professional whether he pays more attention to the organization's vision statement or the leader's behavior. This will quickly illustrate the importance of a clear mental image driving organizational behavior.

The Creativity Approach

Many other training books and programs use a creativity approach. With this approach, the focus is on developing the leader's creative skills. Typically, exercises include activities like brainstorming, discussing stereotypes, and developing different patterns for problem solving. For example, one widely used training program is based on a book that includes exercises that help participants practice:

■ separating themselves from ideal conceptions about reality
■ changing their perceptions of the world
■ thinking about themselves as separate from the objects and situations in the environment
■ shifting their thinking from first to third person
■ creating what is important to them instead of what others expect
■ thinking visually.

This and other programs teach people to be more creative and to create visual images. These are critical skills for project leaders. However, the end product of this type of training is skills that will help the project leaders develop a vision, not the vision itself. Training to develop a vision for a project or an organization requires a more targeted approach.

A Targeted Vision-Training Approach

The visioning approach suggested in this chapter attempts to enhance project leaders' positive attitudes about their projects and their future orientation. It utilizes exercises originally developed for enhancing creative-writing abilities, thereby incorporating the creativity aspect. It is targeted, however, very specifically on current upcoming projects. Rather than trying to turn project leaders into visionary leaders, it assumes that everyone has varying degrees of positivism, future orientation, and creative ability, and presents a method that can be effectively used by anyone for each new project or situation. A study conducted with 114 corporate leaders provided evidence that their visioning abilities increased as a result of participating in this training program (Thoms 1994).

A project leader can use this method working alone. It requires only a large sheet of plain paper, a pencil, two to three hours of uninterrupted time, and a quiet environment conducive to thinking. The environment is important. If the project leader is working in a location where there will be loud noises, interruptions, ringing phones, or visual distractions, this method will not work as well. It may help to dress casually, sit in a comfortable chair, use a table with lots of writing space, and perhaps even play some relaxing music. There are three basic steps: mapping, generating a series of "Wouldn't it be great if ... " statements, and writing the script.

Step 1: Mapping. Put the name of the project in the center of a large sheet of paper. Identify every aspect of the project that you can think of. For example, you would want to include finances, staffing, marketing, and project location. Using a cobweb approach, write each aspect on the sheet of paper, and use lines to show the relationship of each aspect to the others. (See Figure 10 for an example of how this might look.) It is not important that every line be drawn perfectly—a ruler is not necessary. What is important is that every aspect of the project be included somewhere on the drawing. This step helps to ensure that the vision is detailed enough to provide direction to the leader and eventually to followers.

It might be helpful to use a practice exercise before beginning the project vision. For example, take another organization with which you are involved, like your child's soccer league. The aspects that you want to consider would include finances, kids' attitudes toward the program, and location of games.

Figure 10. **Example of clustering for four aspects of a contruction project. Actual cluster would include every aspect of the project and appear as a very detailed web of associations.**

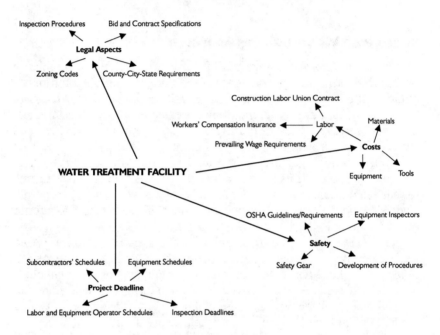

If a project team is made up of members with very specific expertise, or if it will be a self-managed effort, the project manager may decide to involve the team in developing a shared vision. Find a location conducive to open, informal, and relaxed conversations. Be careful about using hotel meeting rooms, as they tend to be uncomfortable. Retreat centers, on the other hand, are often comfortable but may be long distances from home and so inconvenient to team members. If the team is small, the manager's dining or family room may be a perfect spot. Invite people to wear comfortable clothing.

Step 2: Generating a Series of "Wouldn't it be great if ... " Statements. The second step begins by going back to each aspect of the project that appears on the map that the leader, or the team, has created. For each one, generate one or more statements that begin with the phrase, "Wouldn't it be great if ... " For example, go back to the child's soccer league. Some examples of "Wouldn't it be great if ... " statements would be the following.

- Wouldn't it be great if the league had long-term funding and never had to do any more fundraising?
- Wouldn't it be great if all of the kids had fun every time they played?
- Wouldn't it be great if there were no rainouts?

On the surface, these statements may look overly optimistic or unrealistic. The key to this method is that once we have identified the ideal scenario, our planning will take a much different approach. If told to develop a plan for a child's soccer league, most people would simply start by using strategies used by organizers of children's sports programs for generations. They would discuss the budget and fundraising activities. They would discuss rule changes. They would discuss the schedule.

However, when the planners begin with a goal like, "Wouldn't it be great if the league had long-term funding and never had to do any more fundraising?", the planning changes dramatically. Now the leader or the group begins planning a strategy to gain long-term support so that the annual fundraising is no longer an issue. If the planners begin with statements like, "Wouldn't it be great if all of the kids had fun every time they played?", rule changes might include things like, "No parents will be allowed to coach" or "Children may choose a variety of alternative activities besides soccer." The point is that identifying ideal scenarios leads the project in new directions and to heights never before achieved. There may never be a children's soccer league where every child has fun every time, but it is possible to have leagues that are significantly better.

Figure 11 illustrates some examples of "Wouldn't it be great if … " statements for the construction project in Figure 10. Notice that these are very challenging goals. These become the standards that the project leader and the team try to achieve. Think of it as the difference between someone like Walt Disney saying, "Wouldn't it be great if cartoon characters worked at our park?" and "What kind of uniforms should our employees wear?" No, the actual characters do not work at Disney World, but it may feel that way to the visitors. The vision drives planning.

If the project vision is being developed by the project team, the same exercise can be used. However, this is where the leader may need to do some mediation. Some team members will value some outcomes more than others. In other words, Team Member A may say, "Wouldn't it be great if we developed a new software program for the project, which could later be sold as a product?" Team Member B may find that idea unimportant and wants to focus only on the completion of the specific assignment. The leader will only cause problems in the group if agreement on each statement is required. Let the team member who would like to see software development as an outcome take ownership for that part of the vision. Leaders do not need (and hardly ever get) agreement from everyone in their groups or their organizations about what should be accomplished. At the very least, the software program

---

Figure 11. **Examples of "Wouldn't it be great if …" statements for construction project described in Figure 10.**

Wouldn't it be great if we had a complete list of all legal requirements of the project with an indication of the regulatory body and contact person for each?

Wouldn't it be great if we had software that would allow us to track all regulatory requirements as the project proceeds and alert us to any potential problems?

Wouldn't it be great if inspectors from each regulatory body made visits to the site at the appropriate time?

Wouldn't it be great if the project was completed with no labor stoppages or slowdowns?

Wouldn't it be great if all overtime costs could be eliminated?

Wouldn't it be great if all of the equipment necessary for this project were in working condition on the days scheduled for use?

Wouldn't it be great if there were no accidents on this project?

Wouldn't it be great if no OSHA inspections were requested during this project?

Wouldn't it be great if all subcontractors completed their work by the scheduled date?

Once all of the statements are generated, the project team must find ways to achieve each—or at least come as close as possible. In a sense, these are ambitious goals for the project team.

developed for the project will be better than it would have been if a team member had not had a great interest in it.

Step 3: Writing the Script. The third and final step in creating the vision is to pull all of the statements together and visualize the project at the end. One approach to beginning this step is to imagine yourself walking into work while the project is under way. Imagine how the members of the project team are acting, what they are saying, and how they feel. Picture the project and how it looks, how it sounds, the outcomes, the impact on the bottom line of the organization, and the reaction of your boss and your customers to the project. How will you feel? What will you say to the team members? Visualize the best possible outcome for each stage of the project. Many people like to actually write the vision as a script for a movie about the project while it is being completed. See Figure 12 for the beginning of a script for the construction project described in Figures 10 and 11.

Figure 12. Example of how the vision script might begin.

I arrive at the construction site at 8:00 to find work under way. The work site is clean and organized. The subcontractors are approaching the end of their jobs and have met all of the requirements so far. Every worker on the job is working steadily and appears comfortable and satisifed with the materials and equipment provided. All equipment is operating perfectly. A few maintenance people are checking and servicing a crane that will be used the next day. They have requested an OK to purchase a part that looks worn and could cause a problem if not replaced. The county inspector arrives on time with a checklist to OK the last phase of construction. This checklist was provided to us at the beginning of the project, and our site supervisor has already reviewed it and assured us that the project is in compliance with the law and of the concerns that are of particular interest to this specific inspector. There are no fires to be put out, and all of my energy goes into planning and solving a few minor problems related to the steel beams.

As the project leader begins to think about how to communicate the project vision, this script will provide direction. The leader may never share the entire script with all members of the project team, but it will guide her behavior and decisions.

When working with a group to develop a vision, this step will be the most difficult. Each individual will have his own image of the project, based on his own expertise, values, and personal goals. Everyone will picture his role and the project outcomes a bit differently. This is not a problem unless there are contradictory goals. The key is for the leader to make sure that each team member's vision is consistent with the others. For example, if Team Member A is so committed to developing software, she may not complete her portion of the project on time. That will conflict with the leader's vision of completing the project ahead of schedule. The leader has to make sure that everyone is on the same page, so to speak. This may require discussions or even negotiations.

Following a recent successful visioning exercise by a team, one member said, "This can't be our vision because we haven't voted on it yet." The vision developed using this method is not the typical vision statement that will be posted in the lobby or appear on the annual statement. It does not require a majority vote. A vision is a cognitive image that exists in the leader's mind and in the minds of the team members—each in his own form. Team members do not have to agree with a leader's vision. They do, however, have to understand it.

IMPLEMENTING THE VISION

Once the vision has been developed, the leader and the team must begin the implementation process. Implementation is a two-pronged process: communication and planning. Communication must be ongoing, beginning with an initial description of the vision and continuing with day-to-day interactions. Planning will typically be done with the team, developing the strategies necessary to successfully achieve the vision.

Communicating the Vision

The vision must be discussed with the client or customer. The vision must be consistent with the client's needs and values. As explained in Chapter 4, this creates a contract between the leader and the client or organization, which will serve to motivate the leader. Invite the client to the kickoff meeting with the team. In some cases, the client may develop and communicate the vision to the team. In others, the project leader may develop the vision with the client.

At the first meeting of the project team, the leader should describe the vision. It is not important that it even be labeled *the vision*. It is important that everyone on the team understands the standard(s) being set. For example, if the leader's image includes responding to all customer concerns in less than twenty-four hours, that must be clearly communicated to the team. Often the introduction to a new project is done with some fanfare. This does not mean that the leader has to serve champagne and distribute pens bearing the name of the project. What it does mean, however, is that the leader should articulate the vision using motivating language and must help the team see the project as both positive and possible.

Charismatic leaders appear to have a gift for making motivational and inspirational speeches. If a project leader has excellent presentation skills, now is the time to use them. Unfortunately, not all project managers have this gift, but they can still get their teams excited about the project and looking forward to getting started. Models and drawings of proposed projects are one good way to start. It is also important at the first meeting to tell the team how this project is unique and what is in it for the team—for example, "If this project goes well, there will be additional contracts for our team down the road."

The leader must talk to each team member and explain her expectations for each. Since the vision is quite elaborate, she may choose to talk to different individuals only about the aspects pertinent to them. These conversations should provide enough information that the individual understands exactly what the performance standard is. The information has to be communicated repeatedly in a variety of forms. The leader must describe the project vision in newsletters, memos, group meetings, project meetings, and private conversations. The leader should refer to the vision frequently during the planning stages, when giving project assignments and when providing feedback.

Whenever possible, the vision should be linked during speeches and conversations to the values of the team and the individuals on the team—for example, "I know how important it is to you that the environment be protected. This new treatment facility will move our community closer to that goal," or "We are all committed to preventing teen smoking, and this project should cut the percentage of teens who smoke by 10 percent." This builds commitment to the vision, which is important if the leader is to succeed. Occasionally, a project vision will conflict with a team member's personal values. For example, if the project is attacking teen smoking, and a team member grew up on a tobacco farm, that person may not believe in the vision. When this happens, the team member may decide to leave the project. Project leaders should help team members make these decisions. In the long run, the project will be more likely to be achieved when all of the team members share the values that are inherent in the project vision.

Planning in Order to Achieve the Vision

The first step in the planning process would be to develop specific goals that relate to the vision. The "Wouldn't it be great if ... " statements can be used for this purpose. Basically, this will take the leader backward from the overall image of the vision to the specifics identified earlier. For example, if one statement is, "Wouldn't it be great if every child in the soccer league had fun?", the goal would then become, "Every child involved in the soccer league will have fun." If the statement is, "Wouldn't it be great if we could reduce teen smoking by 10 percent?", then the goal is, "Teen smoking will be reduced by 10 percent." A list of challenging goals is identified for the project. Each goal is then addressed during the planning process. The team will have to develop specific strategies to meet each of the goals.

The vision drives planning by changing the psychology behind the planning process. Instead of trying to figure out how to do the job, the planners must figure out how to accomplish the goals. For example, a project team may be in charge of designing the uniforms for all workers in an amusement park. If they do not have a vision and a set of goals guiding the process, they will use traditional planning procedures to choose the costumes. The outcomes may be very nice outfits that reflect current trends, keep costs low, and are comfortable for the employees.

However, if the leader says that he wants cartoon characters working in the park, the project team has to find a way to come as close to that goal as possible. That will lead to solutions like identifying and teaching employees the characters' behaviors, designing expensive costumes that make the employees look exactly like the characters, and developing policies that ensure that the employees are always *in character* when they are in public. Psychologically, the vision and the related goals impact the way that the team approaches the project.

In large organizations, the leader (usually the CEO) may communicate her vision and spend most of her time monitoring progress on it. On a project team, however, the leader usually has a dual role, which includes using her technical expertise to complete certain hands-on aspects of the project. This makes it harder to monitor the team's progress. It is very easy to lose sight of the vision while addressing day-to-day operational issues and completing project tasks. When the project is completed, many project leaders look back and wonder why they did not achieve what they had hoped. Often, the problem was that they lost sight of their original visions.

CONCLUSION

People who are positive about life, are future oriented, and are creative will probably be better at developing a project vision. Although some people may be born visionary leaders, it appears that those who are not can be taught how to develop a project vision. This chapter has explained various vision-training approaches and discussed the strengths and weaknesses of each. The chapter introduced and explained a three-step approach to developing a project vision, which can be used by either a leader or a project team. Once the vision is developed, it can direct the goal setting, planning, and work on the project. This will lead to far greater levels of performance and outcomes than would otherwise be possible.

CHAPTER 6

Leadership and Team Building: Gaining Cooperation from Team Members

YOU ARE A project manager, and you face a *mission impossible*. You must assemble a crack team of individuals, each possessing talents and skills, specialists assigned to a specific task, yet working together as a finely tuned instrument. Each member must possess personal insight drawn from her own functional area, yet develop the ability to gel with others to produce a synergy seen only on … television?

If only life was like television. We would assemble our team, things would go according to plan, and the group would roll off in the van just as the closing credits started to roll. Yet, for too many project managers, forming a team is a mission that they would rather choose not to accept. The difficulties involved in building and coordinating an effective team are daunting. Inattention to these demands has caused numerous projects to fail.

Team building is one of the most difficult tasks that a manager can face; all too often it blows up *in* one's face. What makes this set of duties so frustrating for many project managers is that it is never part of the formal job description. They may come roaring into the project with ideas, energy, personal commitment, and more only to hit a wall before they even get started when they discover that their responsibilities include creating and maintaining the effectiveness of a team of other people. Many managers, uncomfortable with these duties, often are willing to turn a blind eye to them, perhaps under the mistaken belief that the rest of the team are professionals who are willing to put the

Portions of this chapter were adapted from *Successful Information System Implementation* by J. K. Pinto, Project Management Institute: Upper Darby, PA (1994).

implementation effort first and bury personal or departmental conflicts and animosities.

Unfortunately, the reverse is often the case. While nominally being a member of the team, usually composed of members from different functional departments or with varying degrees of technical training, individuals still retain loyalties to the concerns and interests of their own functional departments. Consequently, in addition to harboring prejudices about members of other functional groups, team members will also often view their primary responsibility as being to their own functional group, rather than to the implementation team. This, then, is the challenge that is faced by project managers: how to take a disparate group of individuals with different backgrounds, attitudes, and goals and mold them into a *team* in every sense of the word.

CHARACTERISTICS OF EFFECTIVE TEAMS

A great deal of research has investigated the qualities that effective teams possess and the degree to which those same qualities are missing from less effective groups. While much has been written, there are a great many common aspects of successful teams that these sources share. Briefly, the most common underlying features of successful implementation teams tend to be: 1) a clear sense of mission, 2) an understanding of interdependencies, 3) cohesiveness, 4) trust among team members, and 5) a shared sense of enthusiasm. Each of these factors can be examined in turn.

A Clear Sense of Mission

One of the key determinants of implementation success is a clear project mission. Further, that sense of mission must be mutually understood and accepted by all team members. In fact, research has not only demonstrated the importance of this factor, it has showed that it is the number one predictor of project implementation success (Pinto and Prescott 1988). Team members need a purpose to rally around. They must have some sense of the overall goals that drive the implementation effort. Our professional experiences with project successes and failures have very clearly differentiated the efficacy of team performance in both the presence and absence of overall goals. A further key point is that it is not enough for the implementation team leader to know the goals; this knowledge must be shared by all concerned parties.

A common but often tragic mistake made by many managers—particularly those who are insecure about their authority vis-à-vis the project team—is to segment the team in terms of duties, giving each member a small, well-specified task but no sense of how that activity contributes to the overall project implementation effort. This approach is a serious mistake for several important reasons. First, the project team is the manager's best source of troubleshooting for problems, both potential and actual. If the team is kept in the dark, members who could potentially help, with the smooth transition of the project through participating in other aspects of the installation, are not able to contribute in ways that they may be most helpful. Second, team members know and resent when they are being kept in the dark about other features of the project. Consciously or not, when project managers keep their teams isolated and involved in fragmented tasks, they are sending out the signal that they either do not trust their teams or do not feel that their teams have the competence to address issues related to the overall implementation effort. Finally, from a *fire-fighting* perspective, it simply makes good sense for team leaders to keep their people abreast of the status of the project. The more time spent defining goals and clarifying roles in the initial stages of the team's development, the less time will be needed to resolve problems and adjudicate disputes down the road.

Understanding the Team's Interdependencies

This characteristic refers to the degree of knowledge that team members have and the importance that they attach to the inter-relatedness of their efforts. Interdependence refers to the degree of joint activity among team members that is required in order to complete the project. In many situations, a project team leader may be required to form a team out of members from various functional areas within the organization. For example, a typical IS introduction at a large corporation could conceivably require the development of a team, which included members from R&D, MIS, engineering, accounting, and administration. Each of these individuals brings to the team her preconceived notions of the roles that each should play, the importance of various contributions, and other parochial attitudes. Developing an understanding of mutual interdependencies implies developing a mutual level of appreciation for the strengths and contributions that each team member brings to the table and is a necessary precondition for team success. Team members must become aware not only of their own contributions but how their work fits into the overall scheme of the IS installation and, further, how it relates to the other, necessary work of team members from other departments.

Cohesiveness

Cohesiveness, at its most basic, simply refers to the degree of mutual attraction that team members hold for each other and their tasks. In other words, cohesiveness is the strength of desire that all members have to remain a team. In many ways, cohesiveness is built and strengthened by demonstrating to the team members the advantages that individuals will derive from successful project introduction. It is safe to assume that most members of the implementation team need a reason, or reasons, to contribute their skills and time to the successful completion of the project. In other words, when asked to serve on the implementation team and *actively contribute* to the process, they often first consider why they should do so. It is important not to feel *betrayed* by any initial lack of enthusiasm on their parts, as it is understandable and predictable. Part of the job of a project team leader is to give the team a sense of value, of *why* it should perform to its optimal level.

Further, perceived value directly affects the members' efforts toward establishing a degree of cohesiveness and solidarity as a project team. Project managers work to build a team that is cohesive as a starting point for performing their tasks. Cohesiveness is predicated on the attraction that the group holds for each individual member. Consequently, managers need to make use of all resources at their disposal, including reward systems, recognition, performance appraisals, and any other sources of organizational reward, to induce team members to devote time and energy in furthering the team's goals.

Trust

Trust means different things to different people. For a project team, trust can best be understood as the team's comfort level with each individual member. Further, given that comfort level, trust is manifested in the team's ability and willingness to squarely address differences of opinion, values, and attitudes and deal with them accordingly. Trust is the common denominator without which ideas of group cohesion and appreciation become moot.

Consider the situation of any implementation effort involving personnel from a variety of departments. Conflict and disagreements among team members are not only likely, they should be treated as a given. *Trust* is embodied in the belief of various team members that they are able to raise issues of conflict and disagreement without concern for retaliation or other sanctions. Because intragroup conflicts are so frequent within project teams, the manner in which they are dealt with is often a determinant of the group's ultimate success or failure. In our experience, managers make a big mistake in trying to submerge or put off disagreements and conflict, believing that they are counterproductive to group activities. In a sense, these managers are correct: no one *wants* conflicts among members of his team. On the other hand, we would argue that he is missing the larger picture, which is that these conflicts are inevitable. *The mark of managerial success lies not in dampening conflict but in the manner that conflict, once having arisen, is handled.* It is through establishing trust among team members that conflicts and other disagreements over procedures or activities can be most effectively discussed and concluded with a minimal loss of time and energy.

Enthusiasm

Enthusiasm is the key to creating the energy and spirit that drives effective implementation efforts. The point that the project team leader needs to keep addressing is the belief among team members that they can achieve the goals set for them. This point is best illustrated by an example that one of the authors recently witnessed.

A project leader had been assigned a task and given a team composed of mostly senior, rather jaded, individuals from other departments. Initial enthusiasm for the project was quite low; many project team members claimed that they had seen other examples of this project in the past, and "they never worked before." Despite his initial enthusiasm and energy, the project leader was getting increasingly frustrated with his project team. His chief concern was the constant litany of "We can't do that here" that he heard every time he offered a suggestion for changing a procedure or trying anything new. One Monday morning, his team members walked into the office to the vision of the words *Yes We Can!* painted in letters three feet high across one wall of the office. (Over the weekend, the team leader had come in and done a little redecorating). From that point on, the motto—*Yes We Can!*—became the theme of the implementation team and had a wonderful impact on adoption success.

This story illustrates an important point: enthusiasm starts at the top. If the team senses that the leader is only going through the motions or has little optimism for system success, that same sense of apathy is quickly communicated to the team and soon pervades all of its activities. The team cannot be fooled; it senses when managers truly believe in the project and when they do not.

STAGES IN GROUP DEVELOPMENT

The importance of molding an effective project team is further supported by the work of Tuchman and Jensen (1977), who argue that the group development process is a dynamic one. Groups go through several maturation stages that are often readily identifiable and are generally found across a variety of organizations and involve groups formed for a variety of different purposes. These stages are illustrated in Figure 13.

Stage One: Forming

The first step in group development consists of the stage where there is no group but instead a collection of individuals. Forming consists of the process or approaches used in order to mold a collection of individuals into a coherent team. Team members begin to get acquainted with each other, talk about the purposes of the group, how and what types of leadership patterns will be used, and what will be acceptable behaviors within the group. In essence, forming constitutes the *rule-setting* stage in which the ground rules for interaction (who is really in charge, and how are members expected to interact) and activity (how productive are members expected to be) are established and mutually agreed to. It is important that this step be completed early in the group's life in order to eliminate ambiguities further down the implementation process. In many instances, the role of the team leader will be to create structure to these early meetings, as well as to set the tone for future cooperation and positive member attitudes.

Stage Two: Storming

Storming refers to the natural reaction to these initial ground rules as members begin to test the limits and constraints placed on their behavior. Storming is a conflict-laden stage in which the preliminary leadership patterns, reporting relationships, and norms of work and interpersonal behavior are challenged and, perhaps, reestablished. During this stage, it is likely that the team leader will begin to see a number of the group members demonstrating personal agendas and prejudices (e.g., the conviction by marketing staff that all accountants are *bean counters*). These behaviors are bound to create a level of hostility and conflict among team members that the leader must be prepared to address.

It is also important to point out that the process of storming is a very natural phase through which all groups go. One of the worst things that the leader can do when confronted with storming behavior is to attempt

Figure 13.   Stages in Group Development

Stage	Defining Characteristics
1. Forming	Members get to know each other and lay the basis for project ground rules.
2. Storming	Conflicts begin as members come to resist authority, demonstrate hidden agendas and prejudices.
3. Norming	Members agree on operating procedures, seek to work together, developing close relationships and commitment to the implementation process.
4. Performing	Group members work together to accomplish their tasks.
5. Adjourning	Group may disband either following the installation or through group member reassignments.

to suppress that behavior through ridicule ("Why don't you both start acting like adults?") or appeals to professionalism ("We are all on the same side.") in the hope that members will be shamed or coaxed into dropping the conflict. This approach almost never works because it simply pushes the conflict below the surface. Consequently, team members who have not been allowed to resolve difficulties during an active storming phase may begin engaging in a campaign of guerrilla warfare against each other, constantly sniping or denigrating each other's contributions to the implementation effort. Taken to its extreme, unresolved conflict can sink the implementation process as it reduces the group's efforts to ineffectiveness.

Team leaders should acknowledge storming behavior for what it is and treat it as a serious, but ultimately healthy, sign of team growth and maturation. One of the most productive behaviors that they can engage in is to provide a forum for group members to air concerns and complaints, without indulging in judgmental behavior. The team leader who acts as a problem solver and coach is likely to be far more effective in building a productive team than is the manager who views all intragroup conflict with alarm and actively seeks to suppress it in the mistaken hope that if ignored, it will simply go away.

Stage 3: Norming

A norm is most often defined as an unwritten rule of behavior. Norming behavior in a group implies that the team members are establishing mutually agreed-to practices and attitudes. Norms serve to help the team determine how it should make decisions, how often it should meet, the degree of openness and trust that team members will exhibit toward each other, and how conflicts will be resolved. Research has showed that it is during the norming stage that the cohesiveness of the group grows to its highest level. Close relationships develop, a sense of mutual concern and appreciation emerges, and feelings of camaraderie and shared responsibility are in evidence. The norming stage establishes the playing field upon which the actual work of the team will commence.

Stage 4: Performing

It is during the performing stage that the actual *work* of the project team is performed; that is, the implementation plan is executed. It is only when the first three phases have been properly dealt with that the team will have reached the level of maturity and confidence to effectively perform its duties. One of the most common mistakes that occurs among novice project managers is to push the team immediately into the work of the implementation plan. Typically, this approach consists of holding an initial meeting to get acquainted, parceling out the work, and essentially telling the team members to get started with their piece of the process. The reason that this approach, although quite erroneous, is so often used is the impatience of the top management and team leader to be *doing something*. The real fear that these project leaders exhibit is based on their expectation of retribution from top management and is articulated by the belief that top management expects results. Naturally, this assumption is correct, to a degree. However, bear in mind that what top management is expecting is a successfully completed project. Its rightful concern is with results, not the process. A more seasoned manager, while taking the time to develop a productive team, is also communicating with top management to keep it informed on the progress of team development as part of the project implementation. *It is only when top management knows nothing of what a manager is doing that it assumes that the manager is doing nothing.*

Stage 5: Adjourning

Adjourning recognizes the fact that implementation does not last forever. At some point, the project has been completed, and the team is disbanded, with each member to return to her other functional duties within the organization. In some cases, the group may downsize slowly and deliberately; for example, as various components of the marketing project come online, a team that contains a cost accountant may no longer require that individual's services, and he will be reassigned. In other circumstances, the team will complete its tasks and be disbanded completely. In either case, it is important to remember that during the final stages of the implementation process, group members are likely to be exhibiting some concern about their futures: Where will they be reassigned? What will their new duties be? Project managers need to be sensitive to the real concerns felt by these team members and, when possible, help to smooth the transition from the old team to new assignments.

In addition to presenting the stages in group development, we have also attempted to describe some of the leadership duties for project managers that are a necessary part of their jobs. The *moral* of this message is to pay particular attention to the current stage of team development, and tailor leadership behaviors to facilitate the attainment of that stage. For example, during the early stages of forming and storming, project managers can be most effective when they play the dual roles of developing task assignments, and nurturing and influencing interpersonal relationships. In other words, they need to foster a combination of work and people skills as they set the agenda for the implementation effort within the context of the human interactions that are bound to lead to conflict and disagreement.

On the other hand, later in the team's implementation efforts, the leader can begin to develop a more exclusively task-oriented style. Assuming that the leader has spent adequate time developing the team, by the performing stage, the leader can devote time almost entirely to creating a work-related atmosphere. Finally, in the adjourning stage of the project, leaders should again be aware of and use their people skills as the project starts to *ramp down* toward completion. It goes without saying that this combination of people and task skills is difficult to develop. Further, it is even more difficult, particularly for new project managers, to know when to differentially employ them. Nevertheless, the mark of successful team leaders is often their acknowledgement that the team development process is dynamic, and that their leadership style can and *must* change at appropriate points to address the relevant issues that have surfaced. These issues will be discussed in detail in Chapter 8.

DETERMINANTS OF CROSS-FUNCTIONAL COOPERATION

Earlier in this chapter, we painted a picture in which many project teams are staffed by a skilled but disparate group of organizational members. Because these members come from a variety of different backgrounds and, further, are inculcated with certain beliefs and value sets once they join a functional department, the challenge for creating a viable, cohesive team out of these different individuals is often daunting. So far in this chapter, we have examined the characteristics of effective teams, as well as addressed how team attitudes and behaviors change across various, identifiable stages in group maturation. However, we have not yet examined the basic concern of many project managers: Exactly how does one begin to create cohesion, trust, enthusiasm, and other characteristics of winning teams? In other words, what are some tactics that managers can employ to encourage the type of effective team development so important for project success? The purpose of this section is to report on some of the factors under a project manager's control that can help foster cross-functional cooperation among project team members.

The factors that are discussed below were uncovered as part of a recent research project investigating the causes of cross-functional cooperation on project teams (Pinto, M. B. 1988). The study affirmed the importance of a set of factors that can help encourage cross-functional cooperation and, further, offered some managerial implications that will be discussed below.

Superordinate Goals

Every organization and, indeed, every manager has more than one goal that guides activities and actions. Often, project managers are faced with trying to resolve situations in which team members from different functional areas perceive conflicting goals for a project. For example, consider a common form of conflict between two functional departments: accounting and engineering. For a new product introduction, accounting's primary goal is to minimize cost while engineering's primary goal is to enlarge the range of applications in hopes of increasing client satisfaction and, therefore, use of the project. In order for this development effort to be successful, one functional area may be required to sacrifice, or at least compromise, its primary goals. Aware of these areas of potential cross-functional conflict, managers charged with the responsibility for implementation success are continually looking for ways of developing goals that increase, rather than detract from, cross-functional cooperation.

A superordinate goal refers to an overall goal or purpose that is important to all functional groups involved, but whose attainment requires the resources and efforts of more than one group (Sherif 1958). The superordinate goal is an addition to, not a replacement for, other goals that the functional groups may have. The premise is that when project team members from different functional areas share an overall goal or common purpose, they tend to cooperate toward this end. To

Figure 14. Antecedents and Consequences of Cross-Functional Cooperation

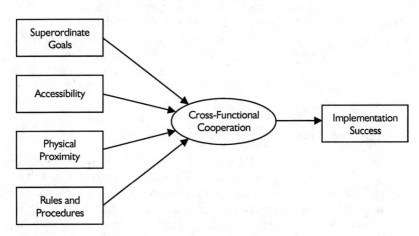

illustrate, let us return to the earlier example of a new product introduction. A superordinate goal for this project team may be *to develop a high-quality, user-friendly, and competitively priced project that will enhance the operations of its customers*. This overall goal attempts to enhance, or pull together, some of the diverse function-specific goals for cost effectiveness, schedule adherence, quality, and innovation. It provides a central objective or an overriding goal toward which the entire project team can strive.

Rules and Procedures

Rules and procedures are central to any discussion of cross-functional cooperation because they offer a means for coordinating or integrating activities that involve several functional units (Galbraith 1977). For years, organizations have relied on rules and procedures to link together the activities of organizational members. Rules and procedures have been used to assign duties, evaluate performance, solve conflicts, and so on. Rules and procedures can be used to address formalized rules and procedures established by the organization for the performance of the implementation process, as well as project-specific rules and procedures developed by the project team to facilitate its operations.

In some instances, project teams do not have the luxury of relying on established rules and procedures to assist them with their tasks. Therefore, they often must create their own rules and procedures to facilitate the progress of the project. Organizational rules and procedures are defined as formalized rules and procedures established by the organization that mandate or control the activities of the project team in terms of team membership, task assignment, and performance evaluation. Project team rules and procedures, on the other hand, refer to the degree to which the project team must establish its own rules and procedures to facilitate the progress of the project. It is likely that greater levels of cross-functional cooperation will result from the establishment of these rules and procedures.

Physical Proximity

Both the literature and common observations seem to suggest that individuals are more likely to interact and communicate with others when the physical characteristics of buildings or settings encourage them to do so (Davis 1984). For example, the sheer size of spatial layout of a building can affect working relationships. In a small building or when a work group is clustered on the same floor, relationships tend to be more intimate, since people are in close physical proximity to each other. As people spread out along corridors or in different buildings, interactions may become less frequent and/or less spontaneous. In these situations, it is harder for employees to interact with members of either their own departments or other departments.

Many companies seriously consider the potential effects of physical proximity on project team cooperation. In fact, some project organizations relocate personnel who are working together on a project to the same office or floor. These organizations contend that when individuals work near each other, they are more likely to communicate and, ultimately, cooperate with each other.

Accessibility

While physical proximity is important to the study of cross-functional cooperation, another factor—accessibility—is equally important. Separate from the issue of physical proximity, additional factors can inhibit the amount of interaction that occurs between organizational members—e.g., an individual's schedule, position in an organization, or out-of-office commitments (Peters 1986). These factors often affect the *accessibility* among organizational members.

For example, consider an organization in which a member of the engineering department is physically located near a member from accounting. While these individuals are in close proximity to one another, they may rarely interact because of different work schedules, varied duties and priorities, and commitment to their own agendas. These factors often create a perception of *inaccessibility* among the individuals involved. Accessibility is defined as an individual's perception of her ability to approach, communicate, or interact with another organizational member.

IMPLICATIONS FOR MANAGERS

The results of Pinto's research study suggest some pragmatic implications for project managers who are interested in increasing the cooperation among project team members.

Cooperation Is a Vital Element in Implementation Success

Cross-functional cooperation can truly result in higher levels of project implementation performance. While this result should not be surprising to most project managers, the strength of the relationship between cooperation and implementation success has important implications. It suggests, for example, that because cooperation is so important for project success, factors that facilitate cross-functional cooperation will also greatly enhance the likelihood of successful project development. In other words, cooperation is more than an element in project success, it is often the key link in helping managers develop a project team that is both capable and motivated to successfully develop the project.

Superordinate Goals Are a Strong Predictor of Cross-Functional Cooperation

Superordinate goals are vital for attaining cross-functional cooperation among project team members. In fact, research has shown that superordinate goals are the strongest individual predictor of cooperation, suggesting that their importance for project success cannot be estimated too highly. The implications for project managers reinforce the necessity of establishing overriding goals, goals toward which the entire implementation team as a whole must work. Superordinate goals are only useful if they require the combined efforts of different members of the project team. If any one individual or subgroup can independently attain the goals, they are not helpful in fostering cooperation. Further, these goals need to be clearly specified and laid out. Excessively vague goals can result in increased confusion, rather than in clarity. Finally, the project manager needs to continually reinforce the pursuit of these goals.

It is important, finally, to note that superordinate goals are not intended as a substitute for other project goals. By their definition, super-ordinate goals are overriding and are intended to complement, rather than replace, other specific project team goals. Consequently, team members from different functional areas may still hold some of their own specific departmental goals, while also being committed to the overall project or common goal of the project.

Set up Policies to Ensure That Team Members Remain Accessible to Each Other

An important way to promote cooperation among members of the project team is to ensure that they remain accessible to each other both during and outside of their regular project duties. Accessibility was previously defined as one's perception of her liberty to communicate with another project team member. A variety of methods can be used to encourage such accessibility, including establishing regular project meetings, setting up formal channels of communication, and encouraging informal get-togethers, e.g., in the hall, over coffee, and at lunch. It is important that team leaders promote an atmosphere in which team members feel that they can approach or get into contact with other team members outside of formally developed hierarchical channels or project meeting times.

Physical Proximity Is Important for Achieving Cooperation

The factor of physical proximity was also found to have an important influence on achieving cooperation. These results suggest that in addition to fostering an atmosphere of accessibility, project managers may wish, under some circumstances, to consider relocating team members to improve cooperation. The importance of physical proximity for cooperation stems from the contention that when individuals work near each other, they are more likely to interact, communicate, and cooperate with each other. Research on the design of the engineering offices at Corning Glass provides support for this claim. As one individual noted: "Engineers get more than 80 percent of their ideas through direct, face-to-face contact with their peers. They will not travel more than 100 feet from their desks to exchange ideas ... and they hate to use the telephone to seek information" (Leibson 1981, 8).

Work to Establish Standard Operating Rules and Procedures for the Project Team

An additional implication reemphasizes the importance of establishing standardized rules and operating procedures for new system implementation. It has been found that rules and procedures can be quite useful in mandating, or determining, exactly how members of different departments and functional areas are required to interact with other project team members. If managers set up standardized rules of behavior, they can better regulate and facilitate the degree and quality of cross-functional cooperation. To illustrate, consider a policy that was instituted by one project manager, which stated: "All major changes to the project, either scheduling, budgetary, or technical, will require input from and active involvement of project team representatives from each functional department." When adequately enforced, this type of operating procedure is a very simple, yet effective, method for promoting cross-functional cooperation.

Because of the relative simplicity of the use of the rules and procedures as a tool for encouraging cross-functional cooperation, some organizations tend to over-rely on this method while ignoring other techniques that have been discussed, such as project member accessibility, physical proximity, or the creation of superordinate goals. While it is true that each of these factors has been found to lead to enhanced cross-functional cooperation, we are not suggesting that project managers choose the technique, or factor, that is most available or easiest to implement. To truly create and maintain an atmosphere in which cross-functional cooperation can take place on the project team, it is highly advisable to make use of a combination of all of the aforementioned factors, including superordinate goals, accessibility, and rules and procedures. Used individually, each may be helpful to the project manager. Used in conjunction with each other, they represent a significantly more powerful tool for creating a cooperative business climate and, consequently, aiding in project success.

CONCLUSION

The purpose of this chapter has been to discuss some of the important issues in developing and maintaining effective implementation teams. Team building and development is an important and ongoing challenge for project managers because, while often time consuming, it can reap large dividends. This chapter has developed a basis for understanding the factors that characterize successful teams. Further, the various stages of team development have been argued to be not only an important, but healthy, sign of implementation team performance. Finally, in an attempt to offer some usable advice to project managers, this chapter concluded with some practical advice on promoting cross-functional cooperation among team members by discussing the results of a recent study that investigated this phenomenon. Experience, as well as research and anecdotal evidence, have long pointed to the fact that the project implementation process is difficult and complex. Many issues and factors go into creating a project team atmosphere that is conducive of successful project implementation. Among the most important elements to be considered are those of team development and cooperation among project team members, particularly when the implementation team is composed of members from various functional departments.

CHAPTER 7

Leadership Ethics: Doing Right While Doing the Right Thing

ETHICS SERVES AS one of the great mantras of modern corporate life. Repeated like some ancient tribal chant by CEOs and consultants, the typical manager will probably hear the term *ethics* more often than the average seminary student will. "Acting ethically," "being socially responsible," and "responding to our stakeholders"—the cries fill our boardrooms, our conference rooms, and our company newsletters, but only rarely are the terms elaborated upon. Like some set of secular scriptures, the organizational mission statement will exhort its managers to act ethically; meanwhile, the CEO will pound away at his pulpit encouraging all employees to take the straight and narrow path to social responsibility (while maximizing profits, naturally). Yet when the sermon is over, the congregation members—pardon me, the managers—are left to ponder the meanings on their own. What does it mean to be ethical? What does it mean to act ethically?

The problem is only exacerbated when the term *ethics* is joined with that equally vague and maltreated term *leadership*. As it has been pointed out repeatedly in the earlier chapters, leadership, as defined by the authors, is more than a gift of divine beneficence bestowed by the gods upon *the chosen ones*. Rather, leadership is an attitude, a belief system, and a set of skills that can be developed like any other talent. Likewise, ethics is more than just a collection of mere homilies. Managers can develop the skills for discerning moral dilemmas, prioritizing various values, and arriving at ethical (i.e., just) conclusions based upon rational reasoning.

The need to develop ethical reasoning skills is especially important in the field of project management. The very same characteristics that make project management such an excellent tool also provide the basis for ethical dysfunction. The world of the project manager is often filled with rapid change and uncertainty, two key ingredients that can lead to moral ambiguity. The project manager, perhaps more than any of his fellow managers, must constantly look ahead, anticipating moral challenges, and providing the ethical leadership for his team and project to survive and thrive.

ETHICS IN BUSINESS

Business ethics is a hot topic. It does not seem that a day goes by without Peter Jennings, Dan Rather, or Tom Brokaw featuring at least one story concerning some aspect of how American business relates with its ethical environment. From the pristine shores of Alaska (the land of leaky tankers) to the shiny office towers of Wall Street (the land of greedy bankers), business is being bulls-eyed as never before.

A major problem confronting business is that outside the government, business is the chief game in town. When a major corporation, its officers, managers, or employees make mistakes, they tend to do it BIG TIME, with lots and lots of press coverage. Ethical lapses by businesses serve forever to tar those companies. Remember Morton Thiokol with its booster rockets, Salomon Brothers with its bond buying, and Ford with its Pinto? Pushing the ethical envelope can have serious consequences, economic and otherwise, for organizations.

This is true for all businesses, no matter what the size. As a manager, you appreciate what your customers and others think of you. An important thing that we all sell is our image. And whether you are the low-cost producer or the premium player in a market, to a great extent the ethical personality you project is going to determine your position in the marketplace. All other things being equal, most parties, whether they are vendors or customers, will prefer to deal with a business and its managers that have a reputation for honesty. Consider the number of parties that you interact with on a daily basis and the possible ethical problems that could arise. Figure 15 reveals just the tip of the iceberg.

A recent Gallup poll shows that the public puts business people somewhere in the middle of the pack in ranking honesty and ethics among professional groups. We rank higher than politicians and lawyers (small comfort, isn't it?), yet not as high as doctors, dentists, and pharmacists. Of course, certain specific business professionals, such as salesmen and insurance agents, achieve far more dubious distinction. The public is demanding more and exerting pressure on all institutions, including business, to clean up their acts.

Figure 15. Daily Interactions for Project Managers

PROJECT MANAGEMENT CHARACTERISTICS THAT MAY LEAD TO ETHICAL DYSFUNCTION

Philosophically speaking, most concepts, belief systems, and technologies are dialectic. That is, the very elements that make something a success can lead to its failure; the positive and negative are inherently intertwined. For example, the internal combustion engine has both positive (increased mobility, enhanced distribution systems) and negative (pollution, monster truck rallies) ramifications. Likewise, the characteristics of project management that make it distinctive and successful may lead to specific problems and ultimately moral dilemmas.

Figure 16 helps to demonstrate the linkage between project management attributes and ethical and project dysfunction. Negative *side effects* can help to produce an ethically inert environment that can further moral vagueness and produce possible problems. Project managers must realize that role overload, hyperactivity, altered structures and systems, riskiness of the project, and unrealistic goals and upper management pressure are parts of the project management landscape that can lead to dilemmas. Recognition of these potential pitfalls is the first step for project managers taking control of their ethical environments.

Figure 16. Project Management Attributes Can Lead to Ethical and Project Dysfunction

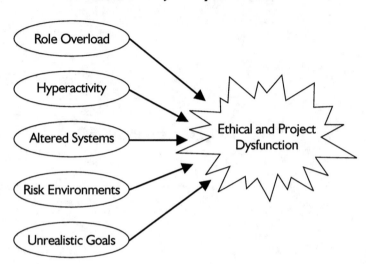

Role Overload

A hallmark of project management is that project managers play many roles: organizer, leader, nagger, boss, tough guy, and exemplar. This profusion of roles allows managers greater flexibility in the formulation and implementation of their projects. But if the number of roles results in confusion and a lack of prioritizing, these multiple roles may actually serve to muddle the perspective of the project manager. As a result, personal goals can get out of alignment with organizational and ethical objectives. This role confusion may often be the first step to either intentional or unintentional malfeasance.

For example, John has the responsibility for verifying his employees' expenses. Due to the severe time constraints of the project, John has found that allowing his assistants (who are on the road quite a bit) to use company vehicles for personal errands to be an excellent motivator, as long as it is "within reason." That is, John has allowed employees to use the company vehicle while technically on company time to run errands and go to doctors' appointments. Yet, company policy clearly states that one can only use vehicles for "business" purposes. In this case, we see two roles, controller and motivator, that seem to be in conflict. Under the unrelenting pressure that most managers face, John has made a decision that has definite moral components. Yet, so harried, he has probably never thought of the long-term ramifications.

Hyperactivity and Superficiality

One of the major characteristics of project management is that of life span. For many project managers, the term *deadline* is especially appropriate. Go past the timeframe contemplated for a project and *bang, you're dead*, at least in an organizational sense. While most management activities have some types of finishing dates, project management is unique in that its very essence is one of time constraint. Think of project management as the tape cassette in *Mission Impossible*—ten seconds, and it self-destructs.

The project manager, as compared to his nonproject brethren, has an extremely hectic schedule. Many activities and functions have to be addressed, and often many are given relatively short shrift. This lack of attention, and the speed at which so many actions have to be completed, limits the amount of time needed to analyze possible consequences. As a result, ethical issues may arise without the project manager ever fully recognizing that the problem was ever there.

Altered Organizations and Systems

Organizations impose structures and systems that reflect their worldviews and priorities. A company that values entrepreneurship will have a different organizational structure than one that is seeking to retain stable markets. A company that is in a highly regulated industry will possess distinct systems from those of an organization participating in free markets. The policies, SOPs, and the hierarchy developed by a company reflect its ethical values. Many firms have well-developed systems for addressing ethical conflicts and these, too, may differ according to how an organization views its attitude toward ethical behavior. Regardless of the ones sculpted, the structures and systems help to link the manager back to the organizational perspective and values, a lighthouse, so to speak, in troubled times.

Project teams can take on a number of forms that reflect the needs of the contemplated project and the parties involved. Obviously, this is one of the great strengths of project management. However, unless the company has a history of utilizing projects, often the structures and systems are created on an *ad hoc* basis. This may work out very well for the project. Likewise, it can result in the structural and systems equivalent of a Frankenstein monster.

The project manager, in creating her project structure, will tend to create a lean, mean machine. In certain situations, this may actually increase the ethical efficacy of the subunit, as the manager creates more direct modes of communication or spawns a more responsive structure.

Yet, there is a danger that in building this new creature, the project manager may cut away at some of the ethical muscle that the organization has grown in order to help police itself.

For instance, consider the concept of formalized hierarchy. We have all bemoaned the slowpoke pace of the *stupid bureaucracy*. Who has not at some point been the victim of some organizational mistake that has arisen *upstairs*. Thus, most project managers, in structuring their teams, will try to reduce the number of levels to a minimum. Yet, a hierarchy does serve important purposes, especially in creating an ethical environment, that allow more objective decisions to be made by mandating a distance between organizational members. A manager in a more formalized relationship with a subordinate will probably look upon his employee's actions in a different light than will one in a more intimate setting.

This is not to say that creating less-formalized structures and systems is bad; obviously, current management theory, as well as commonsense, point toward the simpler organization. In crafting these new structures and systems, the project manager must take care to create alternative means of assessing and protecting its internal ethical environment.

High-Risk Environment

Project managers are constantly on the firing line. Most projects should have a large banner attached, saying: *If I Fail, Go Ahead and Shoot Me*. Projects tend to be highly visible with fairly definite objectives. The simplified project organization structure often has an unintended consequence for managers; there is no place to hide.

Given the potential cost of subpar performance, it is quite understandable that project managers may be willing to bend the rules. Obviously, problems can arise as managers attempt to meet goals in a highly visible arena. Ethical behavior may be the first thing jettisoned in an overheated environment.

Unrealistic Goals and Upper-Management Pressure

Be prepared to give 110 percent. This overused management cliche has inadvertently contributed to countless ethical dilemmas. Realistic objective and goals are essential, not only from a management and control perspective but from an ethical viewpoint. Unrealistic, fairytale goals can lead to managers taking unnecessary risks in order to succeed, and they may have dire ethical implications.

This problem is only accentuated by upper-management pressure to succeed no matter what the costs. The birth of an actual project typically requires that some top-management type championed it. This means that somebody has expended a great deal of political capital, and his butt may be on the line. This upper-level stress on the project manager may be overt or hidden, but it is like the ocean tide—it is always there, exerting inexorable pressure.

WHAT ETHICS IS NOT

One trap that many managers fall into is that of ethical relativism. This holds that ethics is situational and that the appropriate standard of behavior is altered as one changes settings—in other words: *When in Rome, do as the Romans do*. This mode of thinking is often adopted in the business world in the belief that people's ethics can be different in a business setting, as opposed to one's home life. Therefore, misrepresenting your ability to complete a job in a bid is seen as okay since *everybody else does it*. On the other hand, lying in the home front, a different setting, is seen as unethical.

On the surface, this can be a very attractive proposition, since as long as you are following the local customs, you are safe. However, if one merely examines the extreme situations that can result from this line of thinking, the fallacy of moral relativism quickly sets in.

For example, many American businesspeople feel stymied by the Foreign Corrupt Practices Act that bans the use of bribes in securing contracts. Their argument is that their inability to offer bribes hampers their capability to compete overseas, and since so many other countries not only tolerate it but also condone it, the offer of bribes in itself is not unethical in those situations.

Yet, let us expand this situation ever so slightly. In some countries, the purpose of a bribe may be increased from merely giving you an equal opportunity to keeping your competitors out. In some countries, efforts to destroy your competitors' goods may be tolerated as long as the proper palms have been greased. Where does one stop? Unreasonable delays in shipping? Arson? Murder? Obviously, being in Rome does not excuse you from throwing Christians into the lion's den.

Moral relativism is a slippery slope. Whether the setting is in a Third World nation or in the boardroom, the concept that ethics change with the situation is a major-league copout. What it all comes down to is that ethics requires people to draw a line in the sand. Redrawing the line for every situation is not acting ethically.

THE BASIS OF ETHICAL REASONING

Ronnie's company is bidding a new steam-generating boiler project for a large manufacturer of corn products. This project, if won, could be the first in a series of such projects for Ronnie's company. Further, her company has not been doing all that well lately, and upper management has let Ronnie know that they vitally need this *win*. Ronnie has a professional contact with the firm soliciting bids. She calls her friend to get the inside track on what that company is looking for and is given a detailed set of decision specifications that have not been made available to other bidding organizations.

Question: Is Ronnie acting ethically? In order to understand this question, we must first address a broader concept—that of values: What is a value?

Value is one of those overused terms that we just love. Ask a ten-year-old kid, and he will probably tell you that it relates to fast-food menus. Ask a politician, and she will probably tell you that it is a term that goes right after the word *family*. The word has been homogenized and over-utilized nearly to death. Yet, it is an important concept that serves as the basis of understanding ethical reasoning.

A value is essentially a concept that expresses the relative worth or importance of an idea or an object. Values are the basis for all types of decision-making. They help us to try to define problems and serve as gateways to induce more orderly decision-making and, ultimately, a more orderly society. Values serve two basic roles in society and business: decision criteria, and as a definer of sanctions.

Decision Criteria

You like vanilla and hate chocolate. That is a value statement. Values allow us to make shortcuts in most of our decisions. You go into Baskin-Robbins and see two types of people. The first is the person with a well-defined set of values (at least in regard to ice cream) who walks right in and orders vanilla. The other is the person without a clear set of values who insists on getting a sample of all thirty-two flavors.

In business we often categorize decisions as programmed or nonprogrammed. With programmed decisions, the values are so well set that the term *decision-making* is almost a misnomer. In this situation, values providing the selection criteria of the appropriate alternative are so well defined that further debate is often meaningless. Values play a more critical role in nonprogrammed decisions. They provide the necessary basis for making the decision that is unusual and different.

Sanction Definer

By assessing a relative importance to concepts, a value helps to define the punishment or costs when one breaks a rule. For instance, most members of our society have decided that to kill someone with premeditated intent is worse than if one kills in the heat of passion. Thus, the punishment attached to capital murder is harsher than that for manslaughter.

VALUES IN SOCIETY

Values are woven into our society through three basic mechanisms: norms, laws, and ethics.

Norms

Let us assume that you are waiting, trying to get out of a parking lot at an intersection in heavy traffic. The cars are shuffling along, barely moving, extending for miles (starting to sound familiar?). You are in an unfavorable situation because, by law, nobody has to let you out. Yet, invariably someone slows down and waves for you to enter traffic. Why does he do it?

Norms are the unwritten rules that govern most interactions between people in society. Think of the example above. As soon as your fellow motorist slows down and permits you to enter traffic, what do you do? That's right; you wave back in order to express your gratitude. That is another of the norms involved.

How essential are norms? Think once again of driving. We all took driver's education so that we can have an understanding of the laws involved, but the most important rules governing driving are not laws but norms. In the United States, slower traffic keeps in the right-hand lane. Do not tailgate. Allow adequate space between cars. Norms govern 99 percent of all social interactions.

Likewise, norms are the basis of most of our interactions in the business setting. In what order do people speak at meetings? What is the standard delivery date for this type of product? Who puts the new filter in the coffee machine? Norms are so important in business that we sometimes come up with new names for them, such as industry standards. Company policy that typically states suggested guidelines is nothing more than a restatement of important intracompany norms.

Laws

Certain norms are seen as so important that society decides that these should be codified and applied to everybody. One important difference between norms and laws is that of punishment and enforcement.

Norms are values and, as stated previously, values help to define sanctions. Do norms come with sanctions? Of course—next time you are taking a Sunday drive, violate a few driving norms and notice the number of angry stares and gestures you receive. A major difference between norms and laws is that the sanctions applied to violating a law are much more severe and formalized—a jail sentence, for example.

The other important distinction between the two concerns is that of enforcement. Society members enforce norms informally, although the penalties may actually be quite harsh, such as ostracizing. Laws typically have institutional enforcement mechanisms, such as courts or hearing boards, that attempt to implement the punishment in an unbiased manner.

Ethics

Norms that address concepts of basic human concerns constitute ethics. Ethics as a field of study is concerned with determining the *rightness* or *wrongness* of a given decision.

Ethics deals essentially with relationships, two-way interactions between persons living in a complex society. Two essential questions have formed the basis of ethical thought throughout history: What is wrong or right? What is bad or good? As we will discover, a modern approach to ethics addresses both questions.

Is ethics equal to the law? To many managers, equating the two would be a relief. No matter how much we may dislike a particular law, at least such an approach would make it easier to determine the ethical standard in a given situation. In truth, law and ethics often overlap. Some commentators have said that the law is codified ethics. Yet, the question remains—are the two the same?

To answer this, let us get back on the road. You are going about thirty miles per hour when you see that flashing red light, and the police officer cites you for speeding in a twenty-five-mile-per-hour zone. Are you acting unethically? Unless you're driving with your grandmother, most people would probably argue that violating this particular ordinance is not immoral. However, let's say that you are going the same speed on a similar road except this street has a DEAF CHILD sign. This particular law, to drive responsibly in an area with handicapped children, would strike many people as having a definite ethical connotation. On the other hand, a speeding law looks suspiciously like a revenue-raising scheme.

Therefore, when examining what is ethical, do not ignore the laws and rules. Law is a multifaceted construct that serves many purposes. However, for ethical decision-making, use the law as a baseline, not as a substitute for ethics.

ETHICAL DILEMMAS

An examination of ethics must begin with commonsense. Moral commonsense is what your parents taught you, and it has probably served you pretty well. *Share your toys. Do not lie. Be loyal. Keep your promises. Do not go swimming for at least one hour after eating.* These are the basic moral precepts that most people live their lives by. However, a complex world with complex problems can quickly alter your perceptions of these little homilies.

For example, June is getting ready for an important meeting when her copresenter, Ward, calls up and tells her that he cannot attend because he has not adequately prepared. He pleads with her to tell their boss that he is sick. Obviously, June has a problem. On one hand, she has been taught all her life that one simply does not lie. On the other hand, it has also been impressed upon her that she should be loyal to her friends.

This is the essence of ethical dilemmas. What happens when one (or more) principle(s) conflicts with another? Which should we follow? How do we prioritize? Ethical reasoning allows us to address these conflicts in an orderly and rational manner.

MEANS VERSUS THE ENDS

Most ethical dilemmas involve a conflict between the means and the ends. Is it allowable to let individuals suffer if it results in the group being better off? Should we follow basic moral principles regardless of the consequences even if it results in individuals, the group, or the organization being harmed?

When concepts of right and wrong (means) and good and bad (ends) clash, one needs systematic thinking in order to manage the task of selecting the most morally defensible decision. The two must strike a balance.

THREE KEY QUESTIONS

Philosophers have spent the past several millenniums exploring the central questions of ethics in styles that are often enlightening but more often obscuring. Each of these schools has their strengths, but often their philosophical one-mindedness can leave their hapless followers up those famous creeks without those infamous paddles.

A broader approach, as suggested by Bremer, suggests that a sound basis in ethical reasoning can be pursued by addressing three basic questions (1983).

- What is?
- What ought to be?
- How do we get from what is to what ought to be?

What Is?

Typically the most critical question faced by the manager is this one. Determining *what is* can be a difficult process. This is especially so for the project manager, given the constraints that we previously outlined.

This question actually has two components. First, the manager must assess the factual nature of the situation. One must gather pertinent information, which, in itself, can be a difficult thing to do. Also one has to identify the affected stakeholders and assess possible impacts.

Second, the project manager must identify the important controlling values at four different levels: personal, business, professional, and societal. Remember that values are more than just *good thoughts*. Values act as decision rules and provide guidance to the project manager when faced with an ethical dilemma. Violations of stated values have definite real-world ramification. Thus, this four-prong identification is crucial to the ethical process because each level is an important influence upon a leader's actions (see Figure 17).

What Ought to Be?

Whereas, the first question is descriptive, this one is normative and addresses what we earlier called the *ends*. It is essentially a policy question that addresses the ethical concept of doing the right thing.

However, once again conflicting values can make this assessment difficult. For example, Gene is staffing his new team and must pick either Fred or Ginger for a particularly sensitive position. As with many decisions, the *ought to bes* can be numerous and conflicting. Upper management has told Gene that it is important to have a diversified team. Seeking both racial and gender diversity is a goal supported by most organizations. Fred is African-American, and Ginger is female. Both are

Figure 17.   Three Basic Questions

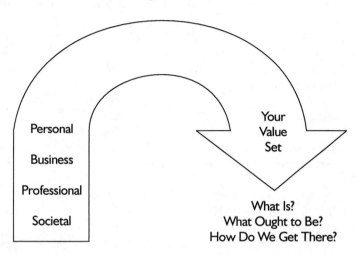

Personal

Business

Professional

Societal

Your
Value
Set

What Is?
What Ought to Be?
How Do We Get There?

well qualified for the position. Which one gets the nod? How does Gene dance around this one?

Probably no part of the ethical decision-making process is as tied to being an effective leader as is determining *what should be*. Creating an ethical vision for your organization or subunit is at the heart of leading wisely. In fact, many have argued that leadership devoid of ethics is not leadership at all.

How Do We Get from What Is to What Ought to Be?

Here is world-class myth #1: Ethics is the sole province of people who sit around all day drinking wine and arriving at great thoughts. Wrong; learning to manage ethically is a lot like learning to drive a car. Remember practicing in your parent's driveway: forward, reverse, forward, reverse? A piece of cake, but as soon as you got out on the highway with cars whizzing past, you really started to worry. The principles are still the same, but, in practice, it becomes incredibly more difficult.

The very complexity of modern life requires that every manager be philosopher and doer. With all respect to the philosophers of old, in today's world the emphasis of business ethics is on the present, and a moving target is always more difficult to hit. Did Aristotle ever worry about meeting a payroll? Did Locke ever sweat to meet a shipping schedule? The business environment makes it much harder to determine how to move from your current state to achieve your ethical vision. Yet, this is the essence of being a good manager.

RELATING THE THREE QUESTIONS

Being effective project leaders requires us to take a complex, multi-faceted world and translate it into something by which we can motivate and inspire. However, simple strategic statements do not mean that a good leader is unidimensional. Rather, he occupies a number of roles. In discussing ethical leadership, each of the three questions puts prominence on a different role.

What is places the emphasis on your ability to see clearly without bigotry and prejudice. To act as a *scout* means that you should be able to move between examining the horizon to looking at the ground only a few feet away from you. This essential role allows you to see without blinders and to alert yourself to potential ethical pitfalls.

The *captain* determines *what ought to be*. This role is concerned with ethical goal setting and creating an effective vision.

Finally, the *wrangler* addresses *how do we get from what is to what ought to be.* This is essentially a strategy question that requires you to formulate and assess alternatives and then implement the most appropriate.

WHAT DOES OUR MOTIVATION HAVE TO DO WITH THIS?

What does it matter what my intentions are? Many managers are pragmatists and identifying the motivation behind their actions is seen as not only bothersome, but as having little value. *Does it really matter whether my motivation for giving to the United Way was because I want to help needy people or because my boss is on my back?*

Once again, we come back to means versus the ends. We can probably agree that, in an ideal world, altruistic intentions should motivate people. But, in our baser real world, are our intentions irrelevant? Carroll suggests that an analogous situation is one to motivating employees. One can take two organizations that have essentially the same employment policies, but in one the workers strive harder because they sense that they are being valued as individuals. In the other organization, the workers know that they are being manipulated and perform accordingly.

But even this explanation seems to fall back on exacting some result to achieve an advantage. Perhaps a better approach is by examining our home lives. Your daughter bounds to you as you get home from work. Would it affect you if you knew that her motivation solely was to get an increase in her allowance? Would you want to be married to a person whose only reason for being with you was because you're a meal ticket? Even the most pragmatic of people would be horrified if these were the motives behind our family members' actions. In this case, the intentions of the parties are paramount.

Thus, the question remains: Why does motivation matter greatly in one situation (home) but matters little in another (work)? Many thinkers and philosophers would argue that intention is the key factor in determining whether an action is ethical or not. In making this determination, one should look at her motivation in deciding whether to act. If the motive is one that would be *just* if applied by everybody, then it is ethical.

CREATING AND IMPLEMENTING AN ETHICAL VISION

Producing and selling an ethical vision is one of the most difficult roles of a leader. When compared to *Let's increase profitability by 10 percent,* a statement like *Be honest in our dealings with customers and suppliers* can seem trite and hackneyed. Part of your job, as a leader, is to make the commonplace and mundane full of meaning. This demands that there must be more than just words. Your public and private actions are the keys to promoting ethical behavior.

Tie Ethical Performance to the Reward System

Many compensation systems unwittingly reward unethical behavior. One must construct these systems with an eye to the future. Remember that the reward system that you create gives one of the most important messages of what you consider important.

Now, in most situations it is difficult or even impossible to directly reward doing the right thing. In addition, many would argue that to specifically reward such behavior does not truly create ethical actions, only responsive ones. Rather the emphasis on how you put together and implement such a system should be on not creating incentive or bonus systems that encourage unethical behavior.

Communicate Your Moral Expectations

Think of the last few meetings that you have attended and what was said. Was anything concerning the right or wrong nature of a situation mentioned? Were the ethical dilemmas of a situation analyzed? Now, one could argue that saying to act ethically is an unnecessary repetition. We are expected to act ethically, so why restate the obvious? Yet how many obvious messages are repeated ad nauseam in the business context? *Increase profitability. Enhance shareholder value. Maximize employee output.* How many times are these and similar sentiments communicated to the organization, the team, and the individual? Repeating the obvious is more than just yadda-yadda-yadda. Rather, it is a statement of values and the priority that the leader places on these values.

Now, are we exhorting project managers to become television evangelists? Obviously not—a balanced approach to communication is important. Teaching, not preaching, is the key.

Focus on the Actual

Even for those managers that make a practice of exhorting ethical behavior, painting with a broad brush can leave a lot of corners untouched. Therefore, it is essential that you couple your more expansive ethical vision with a willingness to explore the ethical implications of actual situations.

Managing ethically is just like any other management situation. As a manager, you must strike a balance between thinking broadly and acting narrowly. But this ability to strike the balance and perceive and act from both perspectives is the difference between the successful and unsuccessful manager.

Be Aware of Potential Ethical Problems in the Planning Stage

Unfortunately, many managers believe that ethics is situational and is, by definition, only something that they can examine in the here-and-now. Make ethical analysis a part of the planning process. This does not necessarily need to be a formal stage in planning. Such formality actually may segregate ethics. Rather, integrate it throughout the process.

Related to this is the importance of scanning the environment. Identification of stakeholders and their values is an extremely important part of this process.

Study and Read Ethics

When it comes to being prepared for moral dilemmas, many managers are Barney Fifes with only the proverbial single bullet in their pockets. Increasing the scope and number of your available ethical techniques requires you to make a concentrated effort. Ethical judgment is like a muscle. Training your moral sense demands that you put the time and effort into it. Is it going to be rock-hard ethical *abs* or a flabby moral belly?

CONCLUSION

The purpose of this chapter has been to discuss the necessity of making ethics an integral part of leadership. Ethics—addressing issues of right and wrong—is one of the three major ways that values are integrated within society and business. Certain basic attributes of project management can result in ethical dysfunction if mismanaged. As a result, active management of ethical issues is a must. Three questions were introduced that permit project managers to discuss and explore ethical issues in an informal and informative manner. Finally, the chapter concluded with some practical advice on tying ethical reasoning to project management.

CHAPTER 8

Leadership and Project Strategy: Driving the Project to Success

FOR MANY PROJECT MANAGERS, running a project is like driving in a blinding winter snowstorm. Hunkered down over the steering wheel, your eyes are focused only a few feet ahead as snow pelts the windshield, and the horizon is only a distant and inconsequential blur. Within such a maelstrom, it is easy to get lost, get out of sync with the organization's purpose, and wander aimlessly down the highway.

Projects have been described as operating within their own little worlds. But what happens when this microcosm fails to connect to its greater universe? Losing sight of top management goals has caused more than a few projects to be canceled before completion. What makes this likely is that the sheer work and detail involved in executing a project allows little time for potential mistakes of omission, changing assumptions, and varying levels of support from upper management.

Many project managers, chosen for their talents in getting things done, are uncomfortable thinking over the wider picture of their projects' places in their organizations' plans, much less puzzling over the dynamics involved. If a potential problem arises, it is often easier just to bull your way through it without much consideration for external players and goals.

Unfortunately, all too often projects take on lives of their own. While other project teams start with a well-defined road and detailed maps, circumstances can make even the most dependable of organizational compasses spin wildly. It is the cultivation of your strategic instincts that makes a difference in effective leadership temperament. Project strategy is more than plotting out your route at the beginning of a journey; rather, it is an ongoing process to ensure that project and organizational alignment is more than a mere mirage, but is a reality. This, then, is the strategy challenge faced by project managers: making sure that the project gets where it really should go, rather than where inertia may lead it. To accomplish this, the project manager must link leadership and management strategies, understand critical project assumptions, identify and surmount roadblocks, and get the team to change course, if needed, along the way.

First, we consider why project managers need leadership strategies to drive their projects to a successful end.

LEADING PLUS MANAGING: STRATEGIES DRIVE PROJECTS

Keeping the project on course requires going beyond the usual project management skills and strategies to exercise leadership strategies. For example, in the Human Genome Project, many external and internal forces, support, and specialized resources are crucial at different times in this project. Strategy research helps explain the differences between times when managing and leading are needed. One way to think of this difference in strategies for a project is presented in Figure 18, adapted for project management from Mitroff (1988, 30). It shows that the project manager's role includes both managing and leading strategies for things that are relatively easy, as well as for things that are fairly difficult to change. We can think of project managers needing to maintain or make changes in key systems, thus splitting the figure into four quadrants. Our focus in this chapter is on the leading strategies, those below the line in Quadrants 3 and 4 (see Figure 18), as other chapters provide good management strategy guidelines. Each challenge and its leadership strategy will fit in the lower section of this diagram.

We now will consider ways of identifying when project systems need leadership strategies to keep them on course.

KEEPING THE PROJECT ON COURSE: SOLVE THE RIGHT PROBLEM, UNDERSTAND KEY ASSUMPTIONS, AND USE NEW FRAMEWORKS

Keeping the project on course is particularly important in volatile, uncertain, complex, and ambiguous environments. Recent changes in managing organizations—such as downsizing, outsourcing, increased reliance on computers and Internet technology, and globalization of what recently were domestic-only markets—put most projects in this environmental context. Since keeping the project on course is easier,

Figure 18.   Managing and Leading Strategies for Project Management

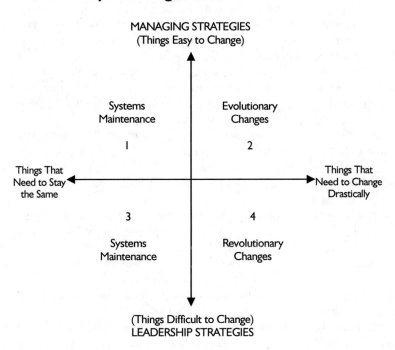

MANAGING STRATEGIES
(Things Easy to Change)

Systems
Maintenance

1

Evolutionary
Changes

2

Things That
Need to Stay
the Same

Things That
Need to Change
Drastically

3

Systems
Maintenance

4

Revolutionary
Changes

(Things Difficult to Change)
LEADERSHIP STRATEGIES

Adapted from Mitroff, 1988.

cheaper, and more constructive than canceling it or making revolutionary changes, we will first review research-based strategies to accomplish this. We suggest three leadership strategies: solving the right problem, understanding key assumptions, and thinking in new ways about the project.

Solving the Right Problem

The first challenge in keeping the project on course is solving the right problem. At first, this may seem obvious, as the project was designed to solve some particular problem. In the project development stage, its specifications and guidelines were written with that problem in mind. But, once the project begins, its details often overwhelm its purpose, and the project team loses sight of the problem. For example, a project team developing a new coating to adapt an existing product for new uses has certain specifications in mind. The project is developing porcelain coating for metal tiles to compete against ceramic-tile and marble-tile products in the building trades. The project begins with the team focused on making a durable coating, without realizing that the actual critical problem will be the adherence of the coating to the metal. While it works on the wear-and-tear aspects, it doesn't even consider that the coating will not stay fixed to the metal tiles.

Most projects start out with specifications and guidelines addressing the problem at hand. From this beginning, there are three possible outcomes: correctly solving the problem (which is the intended result of the project), implementing a faulty or misguided solution to the problem, or solving the wrong problem entirely. Kepner and Tregoe understood that solving the wrong problem well is much worse than poorly solving the right problem (Heller 1990). We here adapt their process of concentrating on *driving forces* to help project managers keep complex interrelated project issues under control.

Applying a driving-forces analysis requires a few relatively simple steps. First, specify the desired outcome of the project. Then, identify what forces affect the successful working of the solution. Finally, ask which force—or forces—is critical. These are the driving forces, and they keep the team traveling toward a successful solution.

An example of a driving-forces analysis is as follows. The coatings project team realized that there were two contrary forces at work in determining the potential success of its metal-tile coating: it had to stand up to outdoor weather, and it had to stick reliably to metal tiles, which are sturdier than ceramic and lighter than marble. Recognizing these driving forces put the team on course to solving the right problem.

Project managers and teams will save themselves much grief if they can keep the driving forces in focus. Considering driving forces is like listening to the weather report, then changing the wipers, filling the windshield washer fluid, or putting on snow tires; you're much better prepared for a safe trip.

Identifying and Understanding Key Assumptions

A second technique for keeping the project on course is to identify the really critical assumptions that support the project. The focus of these assumptions is outside the project, but they may be either outside or inside the organization. Every project relies on key external factors or on organizational resources, which are not under the project team's control; some few of these factors are really critical to the project's success. If these assumptions don't work as supposed, the project will fail. For example, the porcelain glaze project team may solve both its coating

Figure 19. Analysis of Project Core Stakeholders

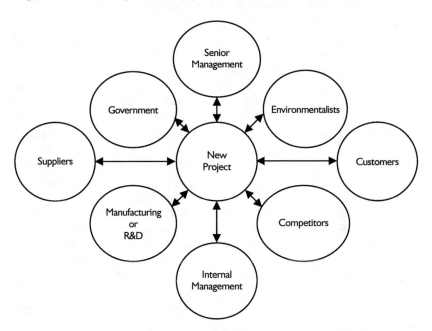

problems, but the primary market for its tile products may be small office buildings, which currently are overbuilt. Or its success may rely on tariffs or duties on imported marble to make the tiles' price competitive. Or it may need critical funds from an obsolete product to pay for the tile firing. It is important to identify and understand these assumptions and their potential impact on the project to keep the project on course.

We recommend a core stakeholders analysis for identifying really key assumptions (Emshoff and Finnell 1979). These key assumptions often are affected by the driving forces just identified. For a project, a *stakeholder* is a group or actor whose behavior affects the ultimate success of the project. Thus, for each stakeholder, the *assumptions* are those behaviors of that stakeholder that would most support the eventual success of the project. Figure 19 shows a diagram of possible core stakeholders for the porcelain glaze project; these include senior management, environmentalists, customers, competitors, internal management, R&D or manufacturing, suppliers, and government. Most projects also have *special stakeholders* unique to the project, which the team can identify. It's worth the time needed for project managers to consider and list a project's stakeholders.

Using their own diagram as a guide, the project manager and key team members reflect which stakeholder behaviors the project's success hinges on most. These become their list of possible key assumptions. They then review each assumption as to its actual likelihood and the potential impact on the project, if that stakeholder's behavior changes. This removes some assumed behaviors, as they are either extremely unlikely or would have no adverse effect if they changed. The team may also consider what other factors or behaviors support that critical behavior's continuance. Sorting out, arranging, and linking the assumptions by their logical connections lets the team build a picture of key assumptions in stakeholder action terms that draws out even the more subtle assumptions. With such a logically linked picture in mind, the team can then target and monitor really critical assumptions and will not be surprised.

For example, when our coatings team began the glaze development, it started chemical analysis, programmed metal supply orders, plus fabrication time and firing facilities. This project's success rested on assumptions about Italian marble resources, continued office expansion, and continuing United States-European trade barriers, among others. These assumptions or stakeholder behaviors relied, themselves, on continued external factors and internal behaviors. If any of these key assumptions turned out to be false, the success of the coatings project might be in jeopardy. The same applies to project leadership. Identifying critical assumptions gives the project manager and team members some critical key issues to monitor to protect the viability and ensure the success of the project. A key assumption that is unsupported can be worse than a spring blizzard or landslide, as the team steers the project to its destination.

Thinking in New Ways

A third way to avoid leaving the road with the project is for the project manager and key members of the project team to develop new ways of thinking about the work and the organization. This is often difficult because the team's focus is on implementing the project as planned. For example, the coatings team had worked two months just developing the specifications for the intended tile product and had been at work on the coating for three months full time. A first suggestion is to review the project in its organizational context regularly. This fits well with the two suggestions above. Taking time to check whether the project, as it is developing, still relates well to the organization's intended purpose (given driving forces and key assumptions) can alert the project manager to potential problems. But, given the project's plan, specifications, and timetable, for many project managers this first tactic would most often involve reapplying enlightened but normal project logic. Research on leadership strategies overwhelmingly suggests changing the framework of reference to get a really new view of the project.

Strategy research points to using frame-breaking techniques and capitalizing on diversity as two useful ways to do this. Mitroff's core stakeholders analysis, applied earlier in the chapter, is a frame-breaking technique; capitalizing on diversity involves establishing and using links to those outside the project team who represent radically different views on the problem and project. Besides their obvious political value, these links are sources of valuable information coming from a very different perspective. The more diverse they are, the more likely that the project team will be able to use these persons and their views to enhance its own thinking about the project, and find out in time about changes in critical issues. The coatings project team linked up with the product team for the supposed *obsolete* product, and found that their estimate of support and resources might be overoptimistic. It reconsidered and began a campaign for separate, noncontingent funding, which it eventually secured.

As an alternate frame-breaking technique, Ramaprasad and Mitroff present a question-and-answer process that the project manager can adapt to get the whole team thinking differently (1984). Their process begins with data, such as a team member's actual project plan details. It proceeds with questions. The first question is "Why?" for each detail, followed by a second "Why" for each answer, until at least two reasons support each project plan detail. The project team then examines these reasons, checking their likelihood and potential impact.

The design of this method is simple to apply, with only two successive applications of the same question, "Why?" to each key project detail. The coatings project team asked why the coating would stand up to outside weather and why it would adhere to the metal tiles. Asking two sets of whys revealed that the adhesive properties of their coating were much more critical than the wear, at this point, particularly when they checked. Ramaprasad and Mitroff point out that people of certain personality types find it easier to use these techniques (1984). This does not mean that only certain people can benefit from these tools, just that some team members may need more practice than others do. Nurturing, developing, and protecting the team's diversity of persons, backgrounds, and opinions are very important to successfully thinking differently about the project in this way.

Thinking in new ways is comparable to putting glare-free coating on the windshield: you can keep the road in view, no matter the conditions.

Once a project begins, adding leadership strategies, such as solving the right problem, identifying key assumptions, and thinking in new ways, to more normal project management strategies can help keep the project on course while also developing team members' broader personal skills. Analyzing driving forces and core stakeholders, using critical review and diverse outside linkages, and successively asking *why* build key conceptual skills. These skills will pay off for the organization in future projects after this project arrives successfully. Keeping the project on course fits into Quadrant 3 of managing and leading strategies (see Figure 18), as it maintains and strengthens key systems. Strategic leadership research also points up ways of identifying and surmounting potential roadblocks to a project.

KEEPING THE PROJECT MOVING: IDENTIFYING ROADBLOCKS

Even if the project stays on course, other factors may interfere with its successful completion. Any project draws important resources in capital, people, and know-how that then become scarce for other managers. It may suffer from the *way we always do it* syndrome if it tackles real innovative changes. Or it may meet the *you can't get there from here* resistance that most project managers know so well. For example, when Florida Power and Light built its St. Lucie #2 plant in only six years, it overcame a hurricane, two strikes, and hundreds of federally mandated design detail changes (Winslow 1984). It seemed that roadblocks shot up around every turn. As mentioned in our Chapter 9 on politics, at crucial decision points in the project, others may attempt to block or cancel the project, and even highly committed team members may feel stymied by the extra effort required. There may also be external adjustments or changes needed for the project to succeed, such as zoning changes, special tax benefits, or official participation by elected officials, and these too may seem insurmountable.

Seeing these roadblocks can be difficult for the project manager and team, as they were not apparent when the project was conceived, and the team is full of day-to-day details to consider. However, they now require attention and action. Potential roadblocks affect viability of the project but (perhaps more importantly) also affect the mindset and culture of the project team. Once the team views the project as really threatened, members may feel stymied and give up. So, rather than being beaten by an outside force, they beat themselves. If the project manager and team don't apply leadership strategies identifying these roadblocks and secure appropriate changes, the project will not arrive at all.

Strategy research suggests several ways to identify and combat key roadblocks to a project. We suggest one way, the Merlin Exercise, adapted from Smith, to help the project manager and team to sort out the real roadblocks from all potential roadblocks and apply leadership strategies to take effective action (1994). As legend recalls, Merlin the Magician was a great help to King Arthur because he knew what was going to happen, since Merlin was living his life backwards. This allowed Arthur to take steps in advance to neutralize his enemies' actions, before the enemies even thought of or took them, thus employing the Merlin factor. To develop the Merlin factor for a project team, the project manager must force the team to think and plan backwards, from the problem solution that the project seeks, to the effective actions needed along the way. The team must try to separate itself from the resources, capabilities, and know-how that it currently has, to open up the opportunities that it needs to capture. This is never easy but can be critical in overcoming the roadblocks and their devastating morale effects. We suggest that the project team follow these simply described but very difficult steps.

First, describe, as carefully as possible, the future state that exists when the project is successfully completed. Then, identify and describe—moving backwards from project completion—each step that successfully occurred to bring about the project's conclusion. Last, for each step and project action, identify any critical resource that's absolutely required. The Merlin Exercise is backward planning with a plus because any and all potential roadblocks to the project are mentally surmounted by the team, and team morale is supported by beginning with success. This is the essence and power of the Merlin factor.

The Merlin factor adapts easily to project leadership, as it makes whatever the project manager and team regard as possible, a potentially achievable target for the project. It reduces potential roadblocks to manageable, rather than gargantuan, size. The Merlin Exercise instills a sense of improvising and adaptation in the team that makes achieving the project's goals doable.

Research by Fulmer and Franklin presents an example of how the Merlin Exercise was used by teams of managers at Hoechst Celanese Corp. (1994). Beginning from the initial vision driving the project, team members wrote statements describing what happens, works, or goes on if the project is successfully concluded. Then, they worked backwards, identifying key milestones that must have occurred, to get to the successful conclusion. The team explored how its strengths and weaknesses will serve it in reaching these milestones and decided how to audit its progress at each milestone. The audit factors may be connected to the driving forces, critical assumptions, and insights identified by core stakeholder analysis.

Adapting a Merlin Exercise to the project team allows for identifying real roadblocks to attaining the milestones, and energizes the team to make changes to surmount them, acting in both Quadrants 3 and 4 of Figure 18. Thus, what might have become a roadblock is leveled and becomes an opportunity.

Applying the Merlin Exercise is like attaching three rearview mirrors to the project so that the driver's field vision is dramatically expanded.

So far, this chapter has considered strategies to keep the project on course by solving the right problem, developing underlying assumptions and logical links, and capitalizing on diversity, plus ways to avoid and surmount roadblocks by thinking backwards. But, even with these protections and precautions taken, the project may still get out of line with external or internal factors of support and finally need revolutionary changes.

Changing the Course of a Project: Revolutionary Changes

Even if the project team stays focused on the right problem, monitors key assumptions, thinks of the project in new ways, and surmounts roadblocks through leadership strategies, it can still can get in trouble from either shifting external forces or internal resource challenges. The project manager who has followed the leadership strategies and suggestions covered here will be aware that this is the case. The final challenge becomes changing the course of the project through totally new terrain so it can arrive successfully. This challenge lies in the fourth quadrant of Figure 18, Revolutionary Changes.

The Merlin Exercise will have helped avoid and surmount roadblocks, but eventually it becomes clear that external forces are so strong, or internal resources are so stressed or challenged, that changing the course of the project is essential. These important deep changes become necessary because external conditions or resources no longer will support the project. For example, when Burlington Northern formed its intermodal project team to develop piggyback *truck trains*, it seriously underestimated the challenge and change necessary. It didn't realize that the team needed to take on Burlington Northern itself to build this new business (Katzenbach and Smith 1994). Its own colleagues' ideas of railroad transportation were the most serious challenge to this project's success. This kind of change is revolutionary change.

Heifetz and Laurie (1997) suggest that change of this kind is very difficult, for it requires two conflicting project team changes in addition to the external actions: The project manager has been accustomed to providing solutions and must now stop this, plus the project team members must now shift out of their follower roles to change. Thus, changing course for the project requires change on two fronts, external and internal. The project manager must stop providing answers and ask the right tough questions; she must wait through the silence and conflicting emotions for the team to develop its own new answers. And, she must keep the process in motion, making team members sufficiently uncomfortable to make real changes, but not frozen in fear. Team and individual attitudes and expectations must change to find and develop different ways of behaving—a completely different team culture. This process of learning to work differently is the ultimate leadership strategy challenge.

This is the most difficult part of project strategy leadership, the real essence of Quadrant 4 in Figure 18. On the one hand, project managers must relinquish their guiding role, so that the team changes its work; but, on the other hand, they must forcefully demonstrate and push hard for what the new project requires.

Research by Taylor suggests that, even though there may be no imminent crisis yet, the project manager must actively apply four tactics (1995). He must demonstrate that current results are patently unsatisfactory (or will be soon) by carefully choosing *competitive benchmarks*, dramatize the need for really new behaviors, openly raise performance targets significantly above normal, and visibly and forcefully lead the project changes.

For example, Rebello reports the project changes at Microsoft to deal with the explosion of the Internet as a good example of these revolutionary changes (1996). Microsoft had plans to build an online service and develop an information superhighway hardware after Windows 95, and this project was proceeding according to plan, but twenty million Internet users had other ideas. The Web was exploding the potential of distributing information, developing knowledge, and linking workers. Microsoft's project was so far behind reality that industry experts wondered if it would be erased as computer users flocked to the Web rather than Windows for information. Beginning with an all-day managers program in December 1995, Microsoft took a massive about-face. The project became the Internet Platform and Tools Division, gathered 2,500 employees within two months, developed alliances with other Web-based firms, acquired software developers, and even wrote and sang grim jingles. This example shows the radical changes that a project manager may need to provoke, support, and sustain, changing the course of a project.

The road to success for a project takes many twists and turns and requires applying leadership in addition to managing strategies. Changing course when absolutely required is like mapping out and taking a detour to arrive at the destination; it requires stopping to make a total change in plans, but the end point reached is still the same. By keeping the project on course, keeping it moving, and completely changing course when necessary, the project manager and team can arrive at a successful conclusion.

IMPLICATIONS FOR PROJECT MANAGERS

This review of strategic leadership research provides useful tools and suggests some pragmatic implications for project managers interested in keeping the project on the road to successful completion, by keeping the wider picture of the project in context in mind.

Apply Leadership in Addition to Management Strategies, as Required

All through the project's development, the highest priority is taken by acting according to its plans and specifications. This will move the project to completion as quickly and efficiently as possible. But, since every project relies on organizational resources, commitments, and skills, plus some suppositions about the environmental context, it may be necessary to apply leadership strategies, as well. Keeping critical support and maintaining key systems may require looking beyond project-specific details and exercising leadership. If the project becomes insupportable due to changes in the organization's environment or resources, leadership strategies are the only way to totally revamp the project.

Understand the Driving Forces, Critical Assumptions, and New Ways to Think about Your Project

Understanding the wider context of a project is not part of a project's implementation plan. Day-to-day activities will get the project successfully completed, but only if critical external forces and necessary resources remain supportive of the project. It pays for a project manager to take time to reflect and use the team to explore those factors that might threaten the project or destroy its usefulness. Strategy research provides tools that a project manager can use to develop the team's understanding.

Think Backwards, Building Team Morale to Surmount Roadblocks

The normal course of a project is frontward through time—from idea, through planning, to development, and finally to implementation. Turning this process inside out to think backwards will do more for the project than just identify roadblocks. It will fire up the Merlin factor and creatively energize the team to foresee and tackle the extraordinary and unplanned. It provides the leadership force necessary to bring a threatened project through.

Don't Give Answers but Do Force the Team to Change Course for the Project, if Needed

Despite the tactics above, it may become necessary to change course and restructure the project, due to external forces or critical resource shortages. Doing this effectively requires a project manager to shift roles, stop answering questions, and begin asking and dramatizing the changes needed. Truly active leadership will allow the project team to revolutionize its project and get moving toward successful implementation.

CONCLUSION

The purpose of this chapter has been to discuss some important issues in getting a project to a successful conclusion. Leading is most often considered an action-oriented skill, but applying leadership strategies can often require some careful reflection. Taking time to reflect, both as project manager and as a team, is an important and ongoing challenge for project managers because, while taking time from direct work on the task, it may ensure the eventual success of the project. This chapter developed a picture of the special purpose of leadership strategies for projects, and adapted and explained some strategy tools and techniques for the project manager and team to keep the project on course, identify and surmount roadblocks, or revolutionize the project, if necessary. Finally, to offer some useful advice, the chapter concluded with some practical suggestions on combining reflection with action. Project experience, research, and anecdotal evidence have supported the fact that just staying focused on the project plan may not be enough. Many tasks and decisions go into getting a project from its go-ahead to successful implementation. Some of the most important tasks may not be direct project tasks at all but rather acts of considering the context, support, and resources on which the project depends so that the project and team can succeed.

CHAPTER 9

Leadership and the Political Side of Project Management

LEADERSHIP AND POLITICS—for many people the two are on the opposite ends of the spectrum. After all, we adore our leaders and hate our politicians, don't we? Leaders are great people. Politicians are self-serving vermin. For our leaders, we want tickertape parades, lucrative book deals, and commemorative statues in local parks. For our politicians, we want speedy court trials and five-to-ten in the state pen.

Obviously, such a simplistic dichotomy quickly proves false because effective leaders are typically adept in the art of politics. Most of us tend to regard political activity with a sort of repugnance, finding the conduct of politicians to be both personally distasteful and organizationally damaging. There is an interesting paradox at work here, however. Common experience will demonstrate to both practitioners and neutral observers that for all our often expressed personal disdain for the exercise of politics, we readily acknowledge that this process is often one of the prime moving forces within any organization, for better or worse.

Political behavior, sometimes defined as any process by which individuals and groups seek, acquire, and maintain power, is pervasive in modern corporations. Examples can include activities as significant as negotiating for a multimillion-dollar commitment of money for a new project, to as mundane as determining who will attain a corner office, to as predatory as the willful attempt to derail another's career, to those as benign as deciding where the yearly office party will be held. The key underlying feature of each of these and countless other examples is that the processes by which we make decisions and seek power, the issues that we deem power laden, and the steps that we go through in order to

---

Portions of this chapter were excerpted from *Power and Politics in Project Management* by J. K. Pinto, Project Management Institute, Upper Darby, PA (1996).

maintain our position often comprise an emotionally charged sequence having important personal and corporate ramifications.

The field of project management is one that is particularly fraught with political processes for several unique reasons. First, because project managers in many companies do not have a stable base of power (either high status or overriding authority), they must learn to cultivate other methods of influence in order to secure the resources from other departments necessary to attain project success. Second, which is closely related to the first reason, projects often exist outside of the traditional line (functional) structure, relegating project managers to the role of supernumerary. Almost all resources (financial, human, informational, and so on) must be negotiated and bargained. Finally, many project managers are not given the authority to conduct formal performance evaluations on their project team subordinates, denying them an important base of hierarchical power. Without the authority to reward or punish, they are placed in the position of having to influence subordinate behavior toward engaging in appropriate behaviors. Consequently, they must learn important *human* skills such as bargaining and influence, conflict management, and negotiation.

Senior and successful project managers have long known the importance of maintaining strong political ties throughout their organizations as a method for achieving project success. Indeed, it is the rare successful project managers who are not conversant in and knowledgeable of the importance of politics for effectively performing their jobs. That point illustrates an important underlying aspect of the characteristics of political behavior: it can either be the project manager's firm friend or her most remorseless foe. In other words, whatever decision one comes to regarding the use of politics in the quest for project success, it cannot be ignored.

This statement does not have to make the reader uncomfortable. No one would argue that project managers must become immersed in the brutal, self-serving side of corporate political life. Clearly, there are so many examples of predatory behavior that most of us are leery of being considered *politically adept*. Nevertheless, the key point is that project management and politics are inextricably linked. Successful project managers are usually those who intuitively understand that their jobs consist of more than simply being technically and managerially competent.

Many companies spend thousands of hours planning and implementing a multimillion-dollar, or even multibillion-dollar, investment, developing intricate plans and schedules, forming a cohesive team, and maintaining realistic specification and time targets—all to have the project derailed by political processes. This is a pity, particularly in that the end result is often foreseeable early in the development of the project, usually as the result of a project manager's refusal to acknowledge and cultivate political ties, both internally to the organization and externally with the clients.

At some point, almost every project manager has faced the difficulties involved in managing a project in the face of corporate politics (Beeman and Sharkey 1987). Recalcitrant functional managers, unclear lines of authority, tentative resource commitments, lukewarm upper management support, and hard lessons in negotiation are all characteristics of many project manager's daily lives. Set within this all-too-familiar framework, it is a wonder that most projects ever get completed.

It is ironic that while project management theory has sought for years to find new and better methods for improving the discipline, power, and political behavior, one of the most pervasive and frequently pernicious elements impacting project implementation has rarely been addressed. Even in cases where it has been examined, the discussion is often so cursory or theory driven that it offers little in the way of useful advice for practicing project managers. Whatever our current level of understanding of power and politics in organizations, we must all come to the realization that their presence is ubiquitous, and their impact is significant. With this acceptance as a starting point, we can begin to address power and politics as a necessary part of project management and learn to use them to our advantage through increasing the likelihood of successfully managing projects.

AUTHORITY, STATUS, AND INFLUENCE

When one examines the sorts of options that project managers are able to use in furthering their goals, it is useful to consider their alternatives in terms of three modes of power: authority, status, and influence. This authority, status, and influence model has been proposed by Graham as a way to make clear the methods by which project managers can achieve their desired ends (1989). The model is valuable because it clearly illustrates one of the key problems that most project managers have in attempting to develop and implement their projects in corporations.

Much has been written on the sorts of power that individuals have. One framework suggests that each of us have available two distinct types of power: power that derives from our personality (personal power), and power that comes from the position or title that we hold (French and Raven 1959). Let us define *authority* as this latter type of power, one that accrues from the position we occupy in the organization (positional power). In other words, the positional power base derives solely from the position that managers occupy in the corporate hierarchy. Unfortunately, the nature of positional, or formal, power is extremely problematic within project management situations due to the temporary and *detached* nature of most projects, vis-à-vis the rest of the formal organizational structure (Goodman 1967). Project teams sit *outside* the normal vertical hierarchy, usually employing personnel who are on loan from individual functional departments. As a result, project managers have a much more tenuous degree of positional power within the organization. Other than the nominal control that they have over their own teams, they may not have a corporatewide base of positional power through which they can get resources, issue directives, or enforce their will. As a result, authority, as a power base, is not one that project managers can rely on with any degree of certainty in most organizations.

Likewise, the second mode of power, status, is often problematic for most project managers. Status implies that the project manager, due to the nature, importance, or visibility of his project, can exert power and control over others in the corporate hierarchy, as needed. Unfortunately, while some project managers do indeed posses an enormous degree of status due to the importance of their projects (e.g., the project manager for the Boeing 757 program, or the project manager for the recently completed *Chunnel*), the vast majority of project managers toil in relative obscurity, working to bring their projects to fruition while receiving little public recognition for their work. Although it would be nice to think that most project managers can rely on status as a form of power and control over resources to enhance their project's likelihood of success, the reality is that very few projects or project managers can depend upon their status as a persuasive form of power.

This, then, leads us to the final form of power or control that project managers may possess: influence. Influence is a form of power that is usually highly individualized. That is, some individuals are better able to use influence to achieve their desired ends than are others. One of the best examples of influence is the power that an individual possesses because she has a dynamic personality or personal charisma that attracts others. For example, well-known athletes are popular choices for endorsing new products because of the personal charisma and *referent* appeal that they hold for the public. Other examples of influence include informational or expert power. To illustrate, if only one member of the project team has the programming or computer skills that are vital to the successful completion of the project, that person, regardless of her title or managerial level within the organization, has a solid base of influence in relation to other members of the project team.

The key point to bear in mind about influence is that it is often an informal method of power and control (Thamhain and Gemmill 1974). Project managers who use influence well in furthering the goals of their projects usually work behind the scenes, negotiating, cutting deals, or collecting and offering IOUs. Influence, as a power tactic, is most readily used when managers have no formal positional authority to rely on. Hence, they are forced to use less formal means to achieve their desired ends. Influence is most widely seen as a power tactic in situations in which there is no obvious difference in authority levels among organizational members.

Developing influence through enhancing our referent powers is a key goal for all transformational project leaders. The larger question, how to enhance referent power, must be considered if we are to improve our abilities to influence others when we lack any formal power mechanisms. Kouzes and Posner have developed a set of leader behaviors all aimed at advancing a manager's referent power (1995). They note that effective leader behaviors include the following.

- Willingness to challenge the status quo—leaders constantly seek to operate in progressive, rather than traditional, modes.
- Creating and communicating a vision—they appeal to their teams through establishing a sense of mission and purpose.
- Empowering others—they give their team members the opportunities and support to succeed publicly.
- Modeling desired behavior—leaders are not hypocrites. If they expect commitment to the project, they lead from up-front, not through driving others to compliance.
- Encouraging others—a key feature of transformational project leaders is their natural enthusiasm and positive outlook. They work to improve their team's commitment through encouragement.

All of the above features of leadership behavior, as identified by Kouzes and Posner, are intended to enhance the leader's referent power and, ultimately, his ability to influence others (1995). It is important to also bear in mind that almost all project teams will have multiple *emergent* referent leaders. There are a number of people who have the ability to influence their peers through establishing some basis of referent power and using it as an informal type of power within the project team. Project leaders should expect to see these people emerge from the team and work with them, rather than viewing them as power rivals. Together, these multiple referent leaders can go far toward influencing both team members and interested project stakeholders in ways designed to enhance the likelihood that the project will succeed.

What is the implication of the authority, status, and influence model (see Figure 20)? Graham notes that the nature of project management work, the manner in which project managers and their teams are selected, and the relationship of projects to the formal organizational hierarchy force project managers to rely to far greater degrees on their abilities to cultivate and effectively use influence as a negotiating and power tactic than either of the other two forms of power. Formal, broad-based authority rarely exists for project managers to use in furthering

Figure 20. The Authority, Status, and Influence Model

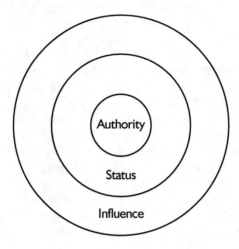

their projects' ends. Likewise, while some projects and/or project managers have the status to gain the resources that they need, it is much less likely that the typical project manager can learn to develop the skills to use influence as a power tactic. The key is realizing that influence is a form of corporate political behavior that can be utilized for the benefit of the project and, ultimately, the organization. In order to better understand the relationship between the use of informal influence tactics and political behavior, we need to explore in some detail exactly what organizational politics implies.

THE IMPLICATIONS OF PROJECT POLITICS

An understanding of the political side of organizations and the often intensely political nature of project implementation gives rise to the concomitant need to develop appropriate attitudes and strategies that help project managers operate effectively within the system. What are some of the steps that project managers can take to become politically astute, if this approach is so necessary to effective project implementation?

Understand and Acknowledge the Political Nature of Most Organizations

Research on politics and organizational life demonstrates an interesting paradox at work: the vast majority of managers hate engaging in political activities, believing that they waste time and detract from the more important aspects of their jobs. On the other hand, these same managers acknowledge that, while they do not like politics, *politicking* is an important requirement for business and personal success (Gandz and Murray 1980). The underlying point is important: we have to acknowledge politics as a fact of organizational and project life. Denying the political nature of organizations does not make that phenomenon any less potent. We realize that, in offering this view, we run the risk of offending some readers who are uncomfortable with the idea of politics and believe that, somehow, through the combined efforts of all organizational actors, it is possible to eradicate the political nature of companies or governmental agencies. Unfortunately, practical experience does not bear out this view; politics are too deeply rooted within organizational operations to be treated as some aberrant form of bacteria or diseased tissue that can be excised from the organization's body.

The first implication argues that before managers are able to learn to utilize politics in a manner that is supportive of project implementation, they must first acknowledge: its existence, and its impact on project success. Once we have created a collective basis of understanding regarding the political nature of organizations, it is possible to begin to develop some action steps that will aid in project implementation.

Learn to Cultivate Appropriate Political Tactics

This principle reinforces the argument that although politics exists, the manner in which organizational actors use politics determines whether or not the political arena is a healthy or an unhealthy one. There are appropriate and inappropriate methods for using politics. Since the purpose of all political behavior is to develop and keep power, we believe that both the politically naive and shark personalities are equally misguided and equally damaging to the likelihood of project implementation success. A project manager who, either through naiveté or stubbornness, refuses to exploit the political arena is destined to be not nearly as effective in introducing the project as is a project team leader who knows how to use politics effectively. On the other hand, project managers who are so politicized as to appear predatory and aggressive to their colleagues are doomed to create an atmosphere of such distrust and personal animus that there is also little chance for successful project adoption.

Pursuing the middle ground of political sensibility is the key to project implementation success. The process of developing and applying appropriate political tactics means using politics as it can most effectively be used: as a basis for negotiation and bargaining. Politically sensible managers understand that initiating any sort of organizational disruption or change due to developing a new project is bound to reshuffle the distribution of power within the organization. That effect is likely to make many departments and managers very nervous, as they begin to wonder how the future power relationships will be rearranged. *Politically sensible* implies being politically sensitive to the concerns (real or imagined) of powerful stakeholder groups. Legitimate or not, their concerns about the new project are real and must be addressed. Appropriate political tactics and behavior include making alliances with powerful members of other stakeholder departments, networking, negotiating mutually acceptable solutions to seemingly insoluble problems, and recognizing that most organizational activities are predicated on the give-and-take of negotiation and compromise. It is through these uses of political behavior that managers of project implementation efforts put themselves in the position to most effectively influence the successful introduction of their projects.

In a recent article on project management and the nature of power, Lovell makes a similar point in arguing that effective project managers must work to maintain constructive political alliances with powerful senior management and influential department managers (1993). He further notes that the persuasive skills and political acumen of a seasoned project manager will allow him to understand and make use of the organization's power environment, the positions of the various stakeholders, and the times and means to develop and maintain alliances, and how to move around political roadblocks. All of these are skills that require objectivity and sensitivity from project managers in order to be done successfully.

Understand and Accept *WIIFM*

One of the hardest lessons for newcomers to organizations to internalize is the primacy of departmental loyalties and self-interest over organizationwide concerns. There are many times when novice managers will feel frustrated at the foot-dragging of other departments and individuals to accept new ideas or systems that are *good for them*. It is vital that these managers understand that the beauty of a new project is truly in the eyes of the beholder. One may be absolutely convinced that a project will be beneficial to the organization; however, convincing members of other departments of this truth is a different matter altogether.

We must understand that other departments, including project stakeholders, are not likely to offer their help and support of the project unless they perceive that it is in their interests to do so. Simply assuming that these departments understand the value of a project is simplistic and usually wrong. One of my colleagues, Bob Graham, likes to refer to the principle of *WIIFM* when describing the reactions of stakeholder groups to new innovations. WIIFM is an acronym that means: *What's in it for me?* This is the question most often asked by individuals and departments when presented with requests for their aid. They are asking why they should support the process of implementing a new project. The worst response that project managers can make is to assume that the stakeholders will automatically appreciate and value the project as much as they themselves do. Graham's point is that time and care must be taken to use politics effectively, to cultivate a relationship with power holders, and make the deals that need to be made to bring the system online. This is the essence of political sensibility: being level-headed enough to have few illusions about the difficulties one is likely to encounter in attempting to develop and implement a new project.

Try to Level the Playing Field

Functional line managers often view the initiation of a new project with suspicion because of its potential to upset the power balance and reduce the amount of authority a line manager has with her staff. To a point, these concerns are understandable. A project team does, in fact, create an artificial hierarchy that could compete with the traditional line managers for resources, support, status, talented personnel, and other scarce commodities. However, it is also clear that organizational realities, which mandate the need for project managers and teams, also need to set these individuals up with some degree of authority or status to do their jobs most effectively.

We have previously suggested that authority and status typically do not accrue to project managers in most organizations. One approach to giving project managers a measure of status vis-à-vis the formal functional hierarchy is to give them the ability to conduct performance appraisals on their project team subordinates. On the surface, this suggestion seems to be simple commonsense and, yet, it is often resisted in organizations. Line managers want to maintain their control over subordinates through keeping sole right to this evaluation process and, hence, may resist allowing project managers this measure of equal footing. Nevertheless, it is a powerful tool because it sends the clear message throughout the company that projects are valuable, and project contributions among team members will be remembered and rewarded (Payne 1993).

Figure 21. Five Keys to Establishing Sustained Influence

1. Develop a reputation as an expert.

2. Prioritize social relationships on the basis of work needs rather than on the basis of habit or social preference.

3. Develop a network of other experts or resource persons who can be called upon for assistance.

4. Choose the correct combination of influence tactics for the objective and the target to be influenced.

5. Influence with sensitivity, flexibility, and solid communication.

Adapted from Keys and Case, 1990.

Learn the Fine Art of Influencing

How does a project manager succeed in establishing the sort of sustained influence throughout the organization that is useful in the pursuit of project-related goals? A recent article highlights five methods that managers can use for enhancing their level of influence with superiors, clients, team members, and other stakeholders (Keys and Case 1990). They suggest that one powerful method for creating a base of influence is to first establish a reputation as an expert in the project that is being undertaken. This finding was borne out in research on project manager influence styles (Thamhain and Gemmill 1974). A project manager who is widely perceived as lacking any sort of technical skill or competency cannot command the same ability to use influence as a power mechanism to secure the support of other important stakeholders or be perceived as a true *leader* of the project team. One important caveat to bear in mind about this point, however, is that the label of *expert* is typically a perceptual one. That is, it may or may not be based in actual fact. Many of us are aware of project managers who cultivate a reputation as technical experts. Unfortunately, in many of these cases, when faced with a true technical problem, the *expertise* that they have taken such pains to promote is shown to be woefully inadequate, perhaps even obsolete. A reputation as an expert is very useful for gaining influence; truly being an expert helps immeasurably with a project manager's credibility.

A second technique for establishing greater influence is to make a distinction between the types of relationships that we encounter on the job. Specifically, managers need to make conscious decisions to prioritize their relationships in terms of establishing close ties and contacts with those around the company who can help them accomplish their goals, rather than on the basis of social preference (Keys and Case 1990). Certainly, there are personality types and interest groups toward whom each of us are more prone to gravitate. However, from the perspective of seeking to broaden their influence abilities, project managers need to break the ties of habit and expand their influence abilities and their social networks, particularly with regard toward those who can be of future material aid to the project.

The third tactic for enhancing influence is to network. As part of creating a wider social set composed of organizational members with the power or status to aid in the project's development, canny project managers will also establish ties to acknowledged experts, or those with the ability to provide scarce resources that the project may need during times of crisis. It is always helpful to have a few experts or resource-providers handy during times of munificence. We never know when we may need to call upon them, especially when resources are lean.

A fourth technique for expanding influence process is that it only works when it is done well. In other words, for influence to succeed, project managers seeking to use influence on others must carefully select the tactic that they intend to employ. For example, many people who consider themselves adept at influencing others prefer face-to-face settings rather than using the telephone or leaving messages to request support. They know intuitively that it is far harder than through an impersonal medium. If the tactics that have been selected are not appropriate to the individual and the situation, influence will not work.

Finally—and closely related to the fourth point—successful influencers are socially sensitive, articulate, and very flexible in their tactics. For example, in attempting to influence another manager through a face-to-face meeting, a clever influencer seems to know intuitively how best to balance the alternative methods for attaining the other manager's cooperation and help. The adept influencer can often read the body language and reactions of the *target* manager and may instinctively shift the approach in order to find the argument or influence style that appears to have the best chance of succeeding. Whether the approach selected employs pure persuasion, flattery, and cajolery or use of guilt appeals, successful influencers are often those people who can articulate their arguments well, read the nonverbal signals given off by the other person, and tailor their arguments and influence style appropriately to take best advantage of the situation.

Develop Your Negotiating Skills

An often-neglected aspect of the project managers' job involves negotiation. They are forced to negotiate on a daily basis with a variety of organizational members and external groups. Nevertheless, with the exception of some seasoned project managers who have developed their skills the hard way, through trial and error, most project managers are inherently uncomfortable with the process. Further, because they find it distasteful, they have never sought to actively improve their negotiation skills or learn new techniques and approaches.

Negotiation is an often distasteful side effect of the project management process. All project managers, in order to improve their influence abilities, must hone their negotiation skills. As part of this task, we need to learn to recognize the tricks and ploys of our opponents who sit across the table from us. Once we learn to anticipate and recognize their techniques, it becomes easier for us to develop appropriate responses, that is, those with the greatest likelihood of succeeding. The key is to use a form of principled negotiation in which you search for fairness, win-win outcomes, and mutually acceptable solutions (Fisher and Ury 1981). A negotiation is not an opportunity to take advantage of the other party. It is a chance to gain the best terms possible for your side while seeking to address the other party's interests, as well. As such, all negotiations should be treated as long-term deals, whether or not this is the case. When we recast a negotiation as a bargaining session between long-time colleagues, it changes the dynamic from one of manipulation and coercion to one of mutual problem solving.

Recognize That Conflict Is a Natural Side Effect of Project Management

Many managers react to conflict with panic. They view any squabbling among team members as the first step toward team disintegration and ultimate project failure. This response is natural and understandable; after all, it is their responsibility if the project fails. As a result, the most common reactions to intrateam conflicts are to do everything possible to suppress or minimize the conflict, hoping that if it is ignored, it will go away. Unfortunately, it almost never does. Conflict, left to fester beneath the surface, is simply a ticking time bomb and will almost always go off at the worst possible time later in the development process. If willful ignorance does not work with conflict, what does?

Project managers need to better understand the dynamics of the conflict process. In fact, we need to recognize conflict *as* progress (Pinto and Kharbanda 1995). The natural results of individuals from different functional backgrounds working together are professional tension and personality friction. In suggesting that project managers adopt a more sanguine attitude about conflict, we are not arguing that all conflict should be ignored. Nor would we suggest that all conflict must be either immediately suppressed or addressed. Instead, project managers need to use their discretion in determining how best to handle these problems. There is no one best method for dealing with conflict. Each situation must be dealt with as a unique and separate event.

Try to Have *Fun* with Politics

On the surface, this principle may surprise some of our readers. We make this point in order to indicate the importance of developing a level of comfort with organizational politics. Successful leaders enjoy the challenge and (for some) even the game of influencing. Certainly it is not something we can willingly avoid, except at a potential cost to our projects. The fact of the matter is that if one is to successfully conclude her project, she must engage in influence and political behavior. This statement is undoubtedly frustrating to some, especially technical experts who often have a worldview that suggests that facts should speak for themselves. The plain truth that we have to understand is that nothing will speak for us and our position quite as well as ourselves— not the facts, nor what is *right* or *should be* done.

CONCLUSION

Politics and project management are two processes, which, while very different, are also inextricably linked. No one can go far in project management without understanding just how far politics will take him in his organization. It is in confronting their frequent failures at getting projects successfully implemented through traditional power means that most managers are forced through expedience to adopt methods for influence and politics. These are not *bad* terms, in spite of the fact that the majority of managers in our organizations do not enjoy employing political means to their ends, and they do not understand the political processes very well. Too many of us have learned about politics the hard way, through being victimized by someone who was cannier, more experienced, or more ruthless than we were. Given that our first experiences with politics were often unpleasant, it is hardly surprising that many of us swore off political behavior.

For better or for worse, project managers do not have the luxury of turning their backs on organizational politics. Too much of what they do depends upon their ability to effectively manage not only the technical realms of their job but also the behavioral side, as well. Politics constitutes one organizational process that is ubiquitous; that is, it operates across organizations and functional boundaries. Politics is often seen as inherently evil or vicious; yet, it is only in how it is employed that it has earned so much animus. All of us, bearing the scars of past experiences, understand the potential for misuse that comes from organizational politics.

CHAPTER 10

Leadership and the Future of Project Management

ONE MESSAGE THAT we have worked to convey throughout this book is the comprehensive nature of project leadership. There is no one face of leadership; rather, leader behavior consists of a huge variety of decisions, attitudes, and actions. This book has shown how leadership behavior can be modeled, and how it allows leaders to formulate and implement visions for the future, build effective and cohesive teams, develop strong ethical decision-making skills, and formulate overall project strategies. Clearly, the idea of a central *role* of leadership in project management is misleading; the reality is that leadership encompasses numerous roles and activities if those leaders are to have the impact that they should.

The other conclusion that all readers should reach has to do with the central importance of project leadership in successful project management. Project management, as much as any activity in our organizations, is a *leader-intensive* undertaking. That is, effective leadership by itself can go far toward ensuring that a project will be a success. Conversely, inadequate or ineffectual leader behavior can often torpedo a viable project even when all other project management activities are performing appropriately. The best scheduling techniques, risk management, scope development, project control, and resource provisions will not ensure project success in the face of poor project leadership. This point was recently borne out quite clearly in a book by Pinto and Kharbanda suggesting that too many organizations spend far too much time in promoting their projects, while at the same time inadequately training and maintaining a cadre of project leaders (1995). The results are counterproductive and wasteful.

What, then, are we to conclude about project leadership? Figure 22 and the following section synthesize some of the key points that we have made in this book and serve as an important starting point for any discussion of

---

Figure 22. Key Points of Transformational Project Leadership

1. Learn the team members' needs.
2. Learn the project's requirements.
3. Act for the simultaneous welfare of the team and the project.
4. Create an environment of *functional accountability*.
5. Have a vision of the completed project.
6. Use the project vision to drive your own behavior.
7. Serve as the central figure in successful project team development.
8. Recognize team conflict as a positive step.
9. Manage with an eye toward ethics.
10. Remember that ethics is not an afterthought, but an integral part of our thinking.
11. Take time to reflect on the project.
12. Develop the trick of *thinking backwards*.

---

how companies can work to better shape their project management futures through first shaping their project leadership training.

KEY POINTS TO REMEMBER

Learn the Team Members' Needs

The first step in effective leadership is to develop an understanding of each individual member of the project team. By understanding, we mean learning as much as possible about what makes each member *tick*, what each craves, what tasks excite each member, what approaches can be used to motivate each member for the tasks at hand, and so on. The key goal of learning members' needs also allows project leaders to serve as developer of their team members by giving individuals the opportunities to grow through learning new skills.

Learning team members' needs consists first of assessing their abilities. Not every team member comes to the project with all of the abilities to perform their tasks. The first task of the team leader lies in accurately determining the status of each member prior to the start of the project. Is additional training necessary? Do team members have a clear under-standing of the roles that they are expected to undertake on the project? How much guidance will be needed during the early phases of the project?

The issue of guidance is important to bear in mind. Research has demonstrated that many project leaders perform most effectively when they understand that their approach early in a project should be more directive, that is, *telling* team members what to do. The directive approach is appropriate here because there is usually a great deal of ambiguity at this point. Team members are uncomfortable with their roles and with each other. Under these circumstances, it is necessary for the project leader to operate as a *boss* until the team has begun to form, and each member has demonstrated the willingness and ability to perform her role. As the project moves forward, team leaders are able to redefine their role relative to the group, moving into a facilitator mode. Team members are now comfortable with their activities and do not need excessive supervision and direction. Instead, project leaders can best serve the project and the team by redefining themselves as *helping* rather than simply *directing*. The focus has shifted from command to one of support.

Learn the Project's Requirements

The primary task of the project manager is to successfully implement his project—period. All activities, like team building, vision creation, per-sonnel training, and so forth are simply steps to better facilitate project success. In order to best ensure that the project can be managed suc-cessfully, it is vital to fully understand the project's special needs. What resources will be necessary to adequately support project development? What are the specific goals and priorities of this project? What are the key risks and scope considerations necessary to understand and facilitate its development? All of these questions must be answered as early in the project as possible.

The project leader, functioning in a proactive way, can force early and complete discussion of these issues. Poor project managers typically operate in a far different mode, one that can be compared to a *ready, fire, aim* attitude. They assume that unless they are *doing something*, the project is not advancing. In fact, it is usually the case that project man-agers who opt for immediate activity are simply setting themselves up for downstream problems. When no effort is made to anticipate future events, including potential problems, the project team is doomed to spending more and more time fighting fires that could have been foreseen and avoided if adequate work had been done up-front.

Act for the Simultaneous Welfare of the Team and the Project

This is the most difficult aspect of leadership—understanding and working to maintain an effective balance between concern for the project team (people) and concern for getting the project completed (task). Balance between these two goals is key. Excessive concern for the task can create tyrants who routinely abuse, hound, and bully their teams into acts of overt and covert resistance, low morale, and lack of commitment to the project. On the other hand, the team leader who displays too much concern for the project team at the expense of the project is also missing the point. True, the project team may love this individual, but the project itself continues to slip further and further behind in schedule and budget.

Research suggests that effective project leaders are typically task driven; that is, they understand that their number-one priority is to complete the project. However, in accomplishing this goal, they also perceive that they cannot do it by simply riding roughshod over their teams. They understand that it is through the commitment and motivation of the team, in fact, that they are able to successfully accomplish project goals. We would emphasize this point: it is *through* the team, not *in spite* of it, that projects succeed. One way that leaders can work to achieve these simultaneous concerns lies in developing goals for the project that satisfy both the needs of the organization and the needs of individual members of the team. Creating challenging and motivating tasks serves the dual purpose of achieving corporate goals for project completion and as team-building objectives.

Create an Environment of *Functional Accountability*

A key leadership role in project management lies in creating a positive sense of team accountability for project success. Rather than members continually pointing fingers at each other or asserting "that's not my job," functional accountability offers project leaders some concrete steps toward creating a spirit of commitment and team concern for task accomplishment. The key steps in developing this accountability spirit suggest that leaders need to do the following.

- Explicitly define and communicate expectations to the team (early and often).
- Increase the validity of the measures used to evaluate individual and team performance. Make sure that the measures are appropriate to the project, meaningful to team members, and accurate measures of performance.

▨ Increase the team's control over its performance (provide resources, structure, and training). When expecting greater accountability from the project team, it is vital that steps are taken to give it the tools to succeed.

▨ Develop meaningful incentives to reward performance. Know your people and what each desires. Give them the ability to succeed and the belief that these goals are attainable through their hard work.

▨ Adjust the accountability *gap*, or range of performance, which is unsanctioned and unrewarded, to accommodate uncertainties in the accountability items above. In those situations where expectations are inherently unclear, or performance measurement is only vague, or the team has less than complete control over the progress of the project, the leader must widen the range of acceptable performance to accommodate these constraints.

Have a Vision of the Completed Project

Too often the activities and outlooks of project managers appear little different from those of their team members. They operate in a distinctly reactive manner—responding to crises rather than anticipating them, and dealing with the project in a disjointed piecemeal approach without conceptualizing its overall scope and goals. We see examples of the results of this mindset every day. For example, in the information systems field (where it is often notoriously difficult to envision completed projects), recent research suggests that over 65 percent of all new projects are late, over budget, and/or nonperforming. Even more damning is the attitude of senior managers in these firms—over 50 percent of those interviewed did not view these numbers as either surprising or necessarily bad. That contributes to a dangerous mindset in which project management is being increasingly confused with systematic *muddling through*.

A far better approach for effective project leaders is to develop a clear vision of the completed project even before the first project-related activities are performed. This vision should be complex and include a visual image of the completed project, as well as links to the commercial or operational side—e.g., how the project will be received by its customers or constituents. When the project vision is thus established, it naturally allows project leaders to begin addressing other key questions, such as how to go about motivating team members, how to ensure that project resources will remain available for its development, and so forth. The vision is key: We can only fully assimilate what we fully understand.

Use the Project Vision to Drive Your Own Behavior

The vision is the metagoal that answers the question: "Why are we doing this?" Coupled with that metagoal are the specific steps we must now take to achieve the vision. The steps taken serve to answer the question: "How will we achieve the vision?" Notice the shift in emphasis: Once the vision is established, it allows the project team and the leader to move from the more general *what* question to the specific *hows* necessary to achieve the project vision. This sequence should occur naturally, as the project moves through its planning cycle into execution. Throughout this process, leaders should frequently return to the vision and ask themselves: "Will this activity help me/us achieve the vision?" and "What else should be done to make the vision a reality?" Notice that the overall vision serves now as the decision source for future activities. When the team is faced with a problem or a series of tough choices, the first key question that should be used to evaluate these alternatives is: "Does this alternative support the project vision?" If the answer is "yes," then the choice is clear.

Serve as the Central Figure in Successful Project Team Development

No project team naturally develops into an effective group. In fact, the reverse is most often true; left to themselves, team members will quickly dissolve into factions, bickering, private agendas, and, ultimately, project failure. This is not a pessimistic view of human nature, merely a natural result of putting members from different functional backgrounds together in a team. These individuals have different goals, timeframes, attitudes, and mistaken beliefs about themselves and personnel from other departments. When they are allowed to bring this psychological baggage to the project team, it is a recipe for conflict. In the face of this conflict, the project leader will either flunk the test, allowing disagreements to disrupt and eventually destroy the team and the project, or the leader will take direct and proactive steps to anticipate conflicts and resolve them effectively.

The key lies in the project leader's understanding of team-formation dynamics. In spite of what we may sometimes be led to believe in the popular business press, it is not natural for people from different functional backgrounds to work together efficiently in a group setting. There are too many points of difference and potential disagreement to ever suppose that effective project teams will naturally evolve. Instead, leaders should make team development their number one priority after the project team has been structured. Once key personnel are in place, it is imperative to begin working with them, one at a time and as a group, to start creating an atmosphere of trust and collaboration. Cohesion does not come about by accident but as the result of serious effort.

Recognize Team Conflict as a Positive Step

It is important to qualify this point. There is a great difference between destructive conflict that arises due to distrust, political scheming, or interpersonal dislike and the healthy conflict that comes about through natural team development. All evolving teams are subject to natural frictions and disagreements. The key often lies in the project leader controlling the team development rather than allowing the team's destructive evolution to control the project manager. The most effective method for controlling this process is to operate in a proactive manner, anticipating the causes of conflict and addressing them immediately.

One of the warning signs of ineffective team leadership lies in how the project manager chooses to address conflicts that develop. Poor managers often panic at the first sign of disagreement among their team members. Their response typically is to suppress the conflict, usually through banal observations, such as: "We are all on the same side." Inattention is not a meaningful or useful response. Left unchecked, unaddressed or suppressed conflict will simply fester and grow until it again raises itself to threaten the project. Some of the poorer project managers can actually engage in several iterations of this *suppress and ignore* cycle in the mistaken belief that they are taking appropriate action. They are mistaken. Successful project leadership consists of recognizing that conflict must be addressed, but in a positive way, so that the sources of the conflict are uncovered and resolved. Only in that way can a project team mature and begin to attain the cohesiveness so necessary for effective project development.

Manage with an Eye toward Ethics

Ethical problems are almost always the result of dysfunctional project management characteristics. When problems are occurring with technical specifications, budget overruns, or customer dissatisfaction, there is a natural temptation to look for ways to cut corners. The worst examples of these practices even involve falsifying data or providing fraudulent information to avoid the penalties of project failure.

What is the answer? Clearly, project managers must examine their project management processes with a critical eye. What are they doing that could potentially lead to downstream problems with the project? What behaviors are they implicitly or overtly encouraging in their project teams? For example, in one project that the authors are familiar with, it became common practice to routinely falsify project performance data in order to cover up ongoing technical problems. When the project prototype was tested by a government agency, these technical inadequacies quickly came to light. Following some digging by government auditors, the whole range of deception came out—padded expenses, false performance results, and so forth. When the case was finally resolved, the offending company was forced to pay millions of dollars in fines, the project manager and several key members of the team were terminated, and the company lost a tremendous amount of goodwill.

In our chapter on ethics, we suggested that while unethical behavior may sometimes appear on the surface as an easy *out*, it invariably leads to even greater long-term problems. Unethical behavior always carries with it costs, some hidden and others immediate. These costs, in extreme cases, have resulted in catastrophic project failures and even death, as inadequate or unsafe projects are introduced or built only to fail, as they inevitably must.

Remember That Ethics Is Not an Afterthought but an Integral Part of Our Thinking

Ethical problems do not arise independently. We need to recognize that, along with the other myriad decisions associated with project management and the operational and economic concerns, there are going to be ethical issues that surface. Treating them as a separate concern makes ethical behavior appear as an afterthought. It is important to understand that the results of each of our decisions as project leaders carry with them potentially serious ethical implications. When ethics are viewed in this light, they push project leaders to frame their decision processes as concerned with making the best possible decision, where *best* is defined to its fullest extent—economically, technically, behaviorally, and ethically.

Take Time to Reflect on the Project

Both the project leader and the team can benefit from taking time now and then to consider the progress of the project. It is more typical of most project managers that they consciously adopt an action-oriented mode during the project's development without devoting sufficient time to considering its overall status. Control information tends to be highly compressed, often consisting of "How's it going?" inquiries, rather than detailed feedback. We suggest that it is both appropriate and necessary for the project leader and team to routinely devote time to objective analysis of the state of the project. These brainstorming sessions can identify looming problems or opportunities, help team members coordinate their activities, and improve team solidarity.

One highly successful project that one of the authors was involved with routinely (once a month) held Friday morning *prayer meetings* in which all relevant project status information was shared with the group. At these fully catered breakfast meetings, the project team leader solicited input from the team regarding upcoming milestones, assessed the state of team member relations, asked for suggestions, and passed along relevant information from top management and other stakeholders. The meetings served the dual purpose of unifying team efforts while forcing members to reflect strategically on the current status of the project.

Develop the Trick of *Thinking Backwards*

One of the best ways to keep the project moving forward is to learn to think *backwards*. In other words, we need to continually assess the project's status in the context of the organization's intended purpose. We must evaluate progress through reunderstanding the project's original goals, i.e., looking backwards to the issues and contexts that drove the project in the first place. When done effectively, this process allows us to continually test our current project assumptions against the original assumptions driving its development. Is the project still fulfilling its original intent? Is the project in its current form still contributing to corporate profitability and strategic direction?

An extremely common side effect of project development in many organizations is to cocoon the project team once it has been given initial go-ahead to act. The effect of this approach is always dangerous; it leads to the potential for well-developed projects that no longer serve a strategic purpose. In other words, we are no longer solving the right problems. The alternative, requiring the project team and leader to continue to think backwards, puts them continually in touch with the larger organization and its goals. The result is projects that have a greater and more immediate impact in the marketplace, or throughout the corporation, because they have been continually reconnected to the company's central mission.

CONCLUSION

Discussions on the importance of effective leadership for project success are likely to continue to grow in the coming years. More and more organizations find themselves adopting project management techniques for their core operations. At the same time, they are discovering that without a cadre of project leaders trained in appropriate project management techniques, they will never achieve anything close to their potential. Both research and practice must continue examining the role of leadership, offering guidelines to project managers attempting to improve their abilities in this key area.

The heartening message that should come across from this work and other texts is that leadership can be taught. It is not simply some innate commodity that one either does or does not possess. The more we study leadership, the more we practice techniques for effective team development and vision creation, the more we operate with an eye toward ethical management, and the greater our abilities grow. This book is an effort to steer project managers toward a greater understanding of the true, multidimensional nature of project leadership. One theme that has run throughout the chapters of this book is that leadership is not a single attribute or characteristic; rather, it is a set of attitudes and determined behaviors, and its very comprehensiveness matches the myriad demands that project management makes on us. Put another way, project management is a large undertaking requiring an understanding of multiple performance expectations. Leadership, likewise, requires us to develop an equal degree of breadth. There is no one leadership style; there is a leadership attitude that affects all subsequent styles that we employ.

It is our hope that readers of this book will see it not as an end unto itself but as a springboard toward investigating further aspects of leadership. In other words, we hope that we have whetted our readers' appetites to explore project leadership in greater detail. What this will require is gaining a better understanding of ourselves, our subordinates, our organizations, and our projects. Effective leadership makes us better, more active learners. It encourages us to critically evaluate our current actions in light of what we seek to accomplish. We hope that this book has begun this process of self-analysis and renewed commitment for a new generation of project leaders.

REFERENCES

Bass, B. M. 1990. *Bass & Stogdill's Handbook of Leadership: Theory, Research & Managerial Implications,* 3d ed. New York: The Free Press.

Beeman, D. R., and T. W. Sharkey. 1987. The Use and Abuse of Corporate Politics. *Business Horizons* 36, no. 2: 26–30.

Bennis, W. 1989. *On Becoming a Leader.* Reading, MA: Addison-Wesley.

Bennis, W., and B. Nanus. 1985. *Leaders: The Strategies for Taking Charge.* New York: Harper & Row.

Blake, Robert R., and Anne A. McCanse. 1991. *Leadership Dilemmas and Solutions.* Houston: Gulf Publishing Co.

Blake, Robert R., and Jane S. Mouton. 1964. *The Managerial Grid.* Houston: Gulf Publishing Co.

Bremer, O. 1983. An Approach to Questions of Ethics in Business. Audenshaw Document No. 16. North Hinskey, Oxford: The Hinskey Sentre, Westminster College.

Carroll, A. 1993. *Business and Society: Ethics and Stakeholder Management.* Cincinnati, OH: South-Western Publishing.

Davis, T. E. 1984. The Influence of the Physical Environment in Offices. *Academy of Management Review* 9, no. 2: 271–83.

DuBrin, A. J. 1995. *Leadership: Research Findings, Practice, and Skills.* Boston, MA: Houghton Mifflin Co.

Emshoff, James R., and Arthur Finnell. 1979. Defining Corporate Strategy: A Case Study Using Strategic Assumptions Analysis. *Sloan Management Review* no. 8 (Spring): 41–52.

Fielder, Fred. 1967. *A Theory of Leadership Effectiveness.* New York: McGraw Hill.

Fielder, Fred, Martin Chemers, and Linda Mahar. 1984. *Improving Leadership Effectiveness: The Leader Match Concept,* 2d ed. New York: John Wiley & Sons.

Fisher, R., and W. Ury. 1981. *Getting to Yes: Negotiating Agreement Without Giving In.* New York: Houghton Mifflin.

French, J. R. P., and B. Raven. 1959. The Bases of Social Power. In *Studies in Social Power,* edited by D. Cartwright, 150–67. Ann Arbor, MI: Institute for Social Research.

Fritz, R. 1991. *Creating.* New York: Fawcett Columbine.

Fulmer, Robert M., and Stephen G. Franklin, Sr. 1994. The Merlin Exercise: Creating Your Future through Strategic Anticipatory Learning. *Journal of Management* 13, no. 8: 38–43.

Galbraith, J. R. 1977. *Organization Design.* Reading, MA: Addison–Wesley.

Gandz, J., and V. V. Murray. 1980. Experience of Workplace Politics. *Academy of Management Journal* 23: 237–51.

Goodman, R. M. 1967. Ambiguous Authority Definition in Project Management. *Academy of Management Journal* 10: 395–407.

Graham, R. J. 1989. Personal Communication.

Heifetz, Ronald A., and Donald L. Laurie. 1997. The Work of Leadership. *Harvard Business Review* (Jan.–Feb.): 124–34.

Heller, Robert. 1990. Sins of Omission. *Management Today* (Feb.): 28.

Hersey, P., and K. H. Blanchard. 1988. *Management of Organizational Behavior: Utilizing Human Resources,* 5th ed. Englewood Cliffs, NJ: Prentice–Hall.

House, Robert J. 1971. A Path–Goal Theory of Leader Effectiveness. *Administrative Science Quarterly* (Sept. 16): 321–38.

———. 1977. A Theory of Charismatic Leadership. In J. G. Hunt and L. L. Larson (eds.), *Leadership: The Cutting Edge,* Carbondale: Southern Illinois UP.

House, Robert J., and Terence R. Mitchell. 1974. Path-Goal Theory of Leadership. *Journal of Contemporary Business* (Autumn): 81–97.

Jago, Arthur. 1982. Leadership: Perspectives in Theory and Research. *Management Science* 28, no. 3 (March): 315–36.

Katzenback, John R., and Douglas K. Smith. 1994. *The Wisdom of Teams: Creating the High-Performance Organization.* New York: Harper Business.

Keys, B., and T. Case. 1990. How to Become an Influential Manager. *Academy of Management Executive* 4, no. 4: 38–51.

Kouzes, J. M., and B. Z. Posner. 1995. *The Leadership Challenge: How to Keep Getting Extraordinary Things Done in Organizations.* San Francisco: Jossey-Bass.

Leibson, D. E. 1981. How Corning Designed a "Talking" Building to Spur Productivity. *Management Review* 70: 8–13.

Lovell, R. J. 1993. Power and the Project Manager. *International Journal of Project Management* 11, no. 2: 73–78.

McAneny, L., and L. Saad. 1997. Honesty and Ethics Poll: Pharmacists Strengthen Their Position as the Most Highly Rated Occupation. Gallup Poll Press Release.

Mintzberg, H. 1994. *The Rise and Fall of Strategic Planning.* New York: The Free Press.

Mitroff, Ian I. 1988. *Break-away Thinking: How to Check Your Business Assumptions (and Why You Should).* New York: John Wiley & Sons.

Nanus, B. 1992. *Visionary Leadership.* San Francisco, CA: Jossey-Bass.

Pareto, Vilfredo. 1897. *Manual of Political Economy.* Reprinted 1970, translated from the French Edition of 1927. Augustus M. Kelly: New York: 211–28.

Payne, H. J. 1993. Introducing Formal Project Management into a Traditionally Structured Organization. *International Journal of Project Management* 11: 239–43.

Peters, M. P. 1986. Innovation for Hospitals: An Application of the Product Development Process. *Journal of Health Care Marketing* 29: 182–91.

Pinto, J. K., and O. P. Kharbanda. 1995. *Successful Project Managers: Leading Your Team to Success.* New York: Van Nostrand Reinhold.

Pinto, J. K., and J. E. Prescott. 1988. Variations in Critical Success Factors over the Stages in the Project Life Cycle. *Journal of Management* 14: 5–18.

Pinto, M. B. 1988. Cross–Functional Cooperation in the Implementation of Marketing Decisions: The Effects of Superordinate Goals, Rules and Procedures, and Physical Environment. Unpublished doctoral dissertation, University of Pittsburgh, PA.

Ramaprasad, Arkalgud, and Ian I. Mitroff. 1984. On Formulating Strategic Problems. *Academy of Management Review* 9, no. 4: 597–605.

Rebello, Kathy. 1996. Inside Microsoft: The Untold Story of How the Internet Forced Bill Gates to Reverse Course. *Business Week* (July 15): 56–67.

Sherif, M. 1958. Superordinate Goals in the Reduction of Intergroup Conflict. *The American Journal of Sociology* 63, no. 4: 349–56.

Slevin, Dennis, and Jeffrey Pinto. 1991. Project Leadership: Understanding and Consciously Choosing Your Style. *Project Management Journal* 22, no. 1 (March): 39–47.

Smith, Charles E. 1994. The Merlin Factor: Leadership and Strategic Intent. *Business Strategy Review* 5, no. 1: 67–84.

Taylor, Bernard. 1995. The New Strategic Leadership: Driving Change, Getting Results. *Long Range Planning* 28, no. 5: 71–81.

Thamhain, H. J., and G. Gemmill. 1974. Influence Styles of Project Managers: Some Project Performance Correlates. *Academy of Management Journal* 17: 216–24.

Thoms, M. A. 1994. A Study of Future Time Perspective as a Determinant of Visioning Skill and the Impact of Training on Visioning Skill. Unpublished doctoral dissertation, The Ohio State University, Columbus, OH.

Thoms, P., and M. A. Govekar. In Press. Vision Is in the Eyes of the Leader: A Control Theory Model Explaining Organizational Vision. *OD Practitioner.*

Tuchman, B. W., and M. A. Jensen. 1977. Stages in Small Group Development Revisited. *Group and Organizational Studies* 2: 419–27.

The U.S. Must Do as GM Has Done. 1989. *Fortune* (Feb.): 70–79.

Vroom, Victor H. 1964. *Work and Motivation.* New York: John Wiley & Sons.

Vroom, Victor H., and Arthur G. Jago. 1988. *The New Leadership: Managing Participation in Organizations.* Englewood Cliffs, NJ: Prentice–Hall.

———. 1988. Managing Participation: A Critical Dimension of Leadership. *Journal of Management Development* 7, no. 5: 32–42.

Vroom, Victor H., and Philip W. Yetton. 1973. *Leadership and Decision-Making.* Pittsburgh, PA: University of Pittsburgh Press.

Vroom, V. H., P. W. Yetton, and A. G. Jago. 1976. *Leadership and Decision-Making Cases and Manuals for Use in Leadership Training,* 3d ed. New Haven, CT: Authors.

Winslow, Ron. 1984. Utility Cuts Red Tape, Builds Nuclear Plant Almost on Schedule. *Wall Street Journal* (Feb. 22): a18.